Colborne Ontario and Area in Colour Photos, Saving Our History One Photo at a Time

Photography
by Barbara Raué
©2019

Series Name: Cruising Ontario

Book 223: Colborne, Castleton, King City, Nobleton

Cover photo: 8 Victory Street, Page 33

©All the photos in this book have been taken with my cameras. I own the rights to them.

Series Name: Cruising Ontario
Saving Our History One Photo at a Time
in colour photos

Books Available in Alphabetical Order:
Aberfoyle, Acton, Ajax, Alton, Amherstburg, Ancaster, Arthur, Auburn, Aylmer, Ayr, Beaver Valley, Belgrave, Belleville, Bloomingdale, Blyth, Brantford, Brockville, Burford, Burlington, Caledon, Caledonia, Cambridge, Carlow, Chatsworth, Clifford, Collingwood, Conestogo, Delhi, Dorchester to Aylmer, Drayton, Drumbo, Dundas, Dunlop, Eden Mills, Elmira, Elora, Erin, Essex, Fergus, Goderich, Grimsby, Guelph, Hagersville, Hamilton, Hanover, Harriston, Hespeler, Jarvis, Kingston, Kingsville, Kitchener, Lake Superior, Lincoln, Linwood, Listowel, London, Lucknow, Merrickville, Mono, Mount Forest, Mount Pleasant, Neustadt, New Hamburg, Newboro, Newport, Niagara-on-the-Lake, Niagara Falls, North Bay, Oakville, Onondaga, Orangeville, Orillia, Oshawa, Owen Sound, Palmerston, Paris, Pelham, Perth, Peterborough, Petrolia, Pickering, Port Colborne, Port Elgin, Portland, Preston, Rockwood, Sarnia, Sault Ste. Marie, Seaforth, Sheffield, Shelburne, Simcoe, Smiths Falls, Smithville, Southampton, St. Catharines, St. George, St. Jacobs, St. Marys, St. Thomas, Stoney Creek, Stratford, Thamesford, Thunder Bay, Tillsonburg, Toronto, Waterdown, Waterford, Waterloo, Welland, Wellesley, West Flamborough, Westport, Whitby, Windsor, Wingham, Woodstock

Book 211: Fort Erie
Book 212-215 Haldimand County
Book 216: Sudbury
Book 217: Parry Sound
Book 218-219: Uxbridge
Book 220: Port Perry
Book 221-222: Stouffville
Book 223: Colborne

Table of Contents

Colborne	Page 5
Rice Lake – Gores Landing	Page 52
Castleton	Page 56
Wicklow	Page 61
King City	Page 63
Nobleton	Page 69

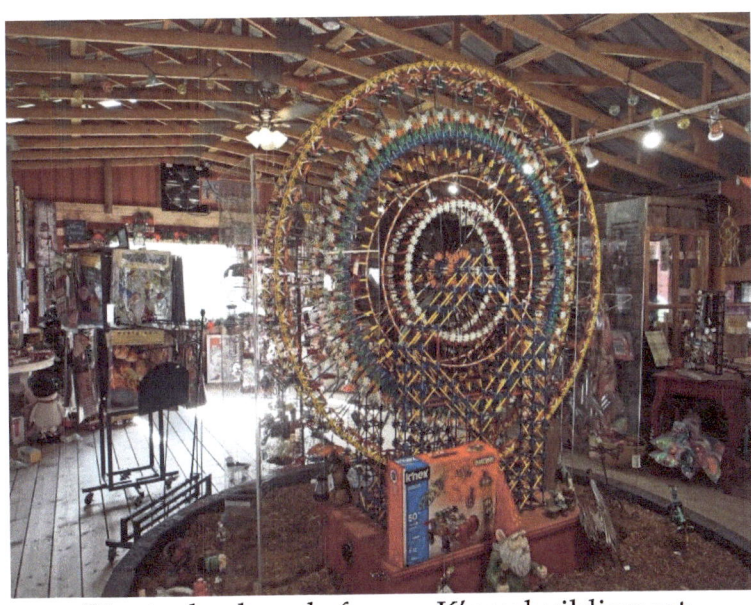

Giant wheel made from a K'nex building set

Cramahe Township was established in 1792. Joseph Abbott Keeler, son of the first settler of Cramahe Township, founded the village of Colborne in 1815 when he opened the first store and post office. He had the village surveyed, laid out the public square and donated the land.

Joseph Keeler (1770-1839) was the first settler who landed on the shores of Cramahe Township with forty United Empire Loyalist families from Rutland, Vermont. Keeler, his son Joseph Abbott Keeler (1788-1855) and his grandson Joseph Keeler (1824-1881) were instrumental in establishing the settlements at Lakeport, Colborne and Castleton.

A store established in Colborne in about 1819 by Joseph Keeler provided the nucleus around which a small community began to develop. Within ten years, a distillery and a blacksmith's shop had been erected. Colborne was named after Lieutenant Governor Sir John Colborne. With the establishment of a harbor nearby for the shipment of lumber and grain, Colborne prospered. By 1846, it contained a foundry, a pottery, six stores, three churches, tradesmen and artisans, and about four hundred residents. The arrival of the Grand Trunk Railway in 1856, spurred further growth.

In 2001, Colborne and Cramahe Township were amalgamated as part of municipal restructuring to form an expanded Township of Cramahe.

Colborne is the home of the Big Apple, a tourist attraction located along Highway 401. The Big Apple is 10.7 meters (35 feet) tall and has a diameter of 11.6 meters (38 feet) - the largest apple in the world. There is an observation deck on top of the apple, and adjacent to it is a restaurant and a store to buy all your apple treats.

King City is the largest community in King Township in York Region north of Toronto. In 1836, a settlement styled *Springhill* was established in King. With the arrival of the Ontario, Simcoe and Huron Railway in 1853, the settlement began to expand. In 1890, the reeve of King Township James Whiting Crossley incorporated King City by merging the hamlets of Springhill, Kinghorn, Laskay, and Eversley. King City is characterized by rolling hills and clustered temperate forests. Many lakes and ponds dot the area. Creeks and streams from King City, the surrounding area, and as far west as Bolton and as far east as Stouffville are the origin for the East Humber River.

The King Township Museum in King City is a local history museum for the township of King at 2920 King Road. The museum consists of a building which houses the majority of collections held. This building was originally built in 1861 as the site of the Kinghorn School SS #23. It was updated and expanded in 1958 and again in 1963, and purchased by the township in 1978. The King Township Historical Society established the museum in 1979 and opened it in 1982.

The village of Nobleton is located in southwestern King Township and is surrounded by hills and forests. It was named after Joseph Noble and began as a settlement in about 1812. Most of the early settlers came from England, Scotland and Ireland. There are many horse farms here. The Humber River flows through the town. Nobleton was first settled in 1812, primarily based on its location midway between King City and Bolton on the east–west route, and Kleinburg and Schomberg on the north–south route. Taverns and hotels were built to serve travellers, and general stores and a post office were built to serve the fledgling businesses.

Colborne

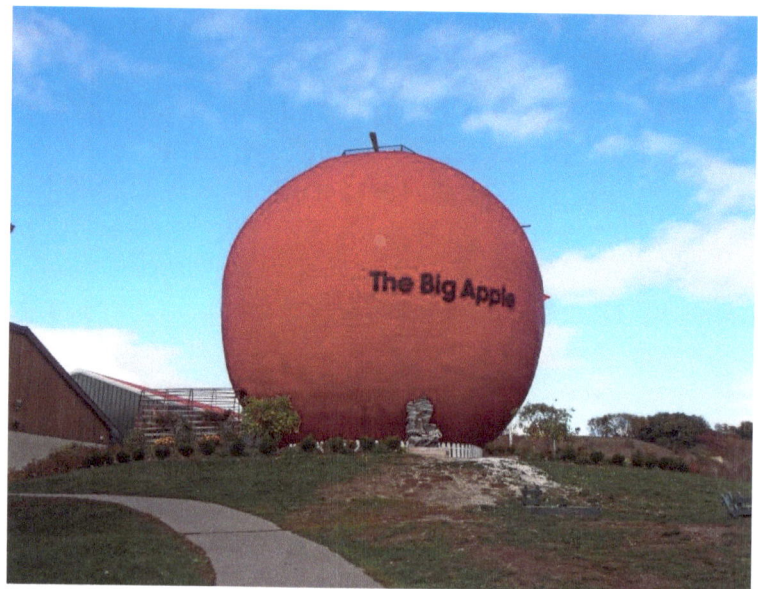

The Big Apple

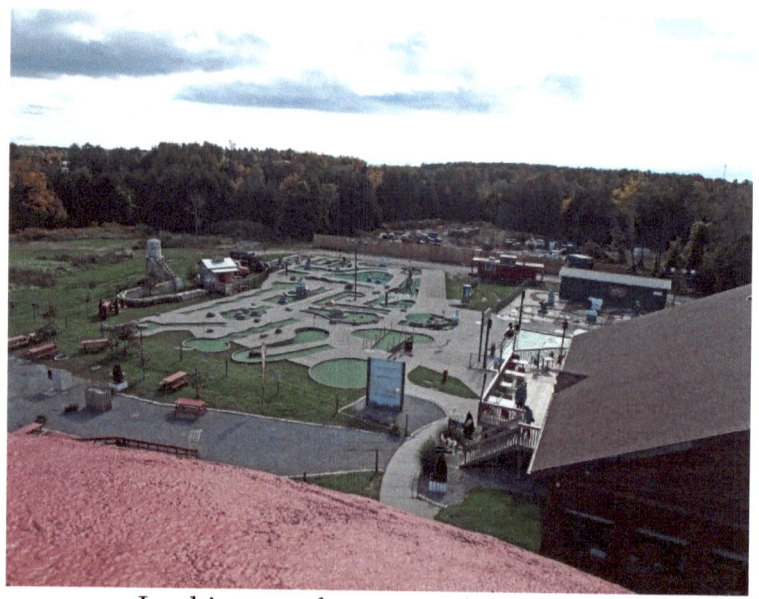

Looking out from top of Big Apple

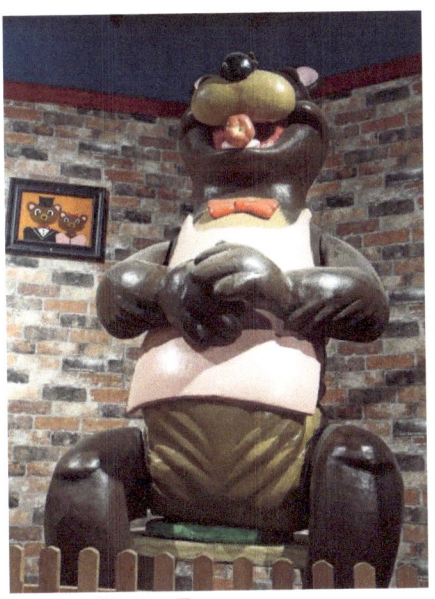
Papa Bear

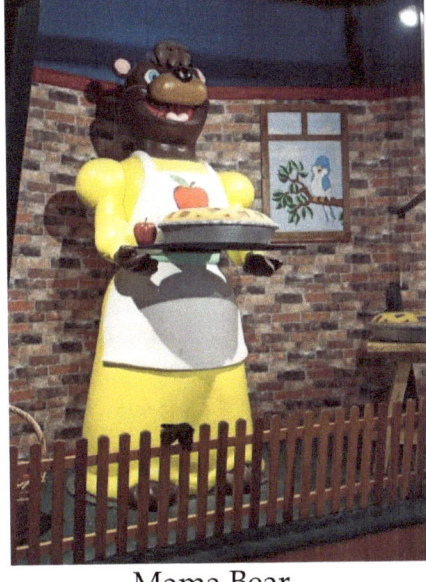
Mama Bear

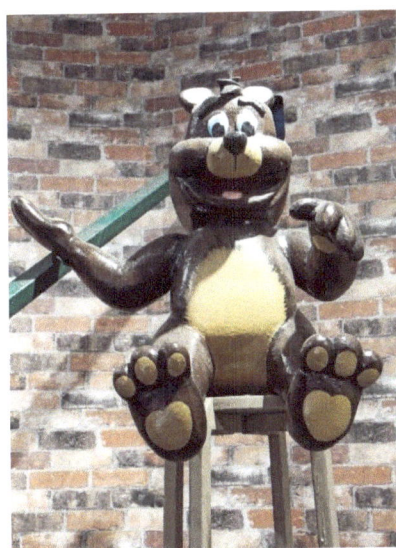
Baby Bear

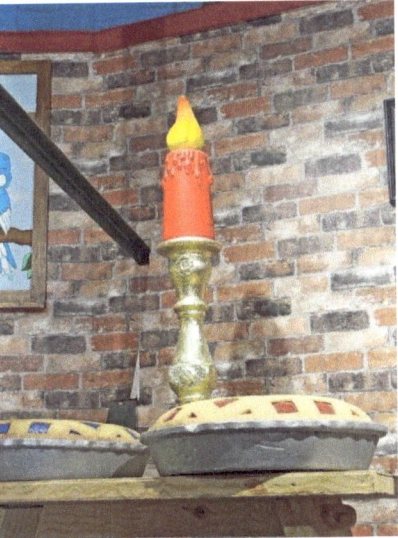
Pies cooling

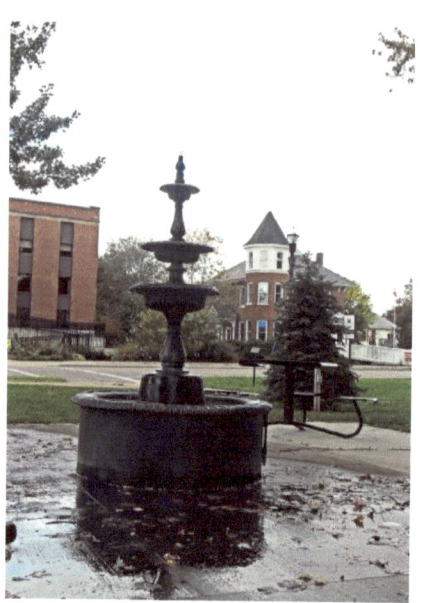
Fountain

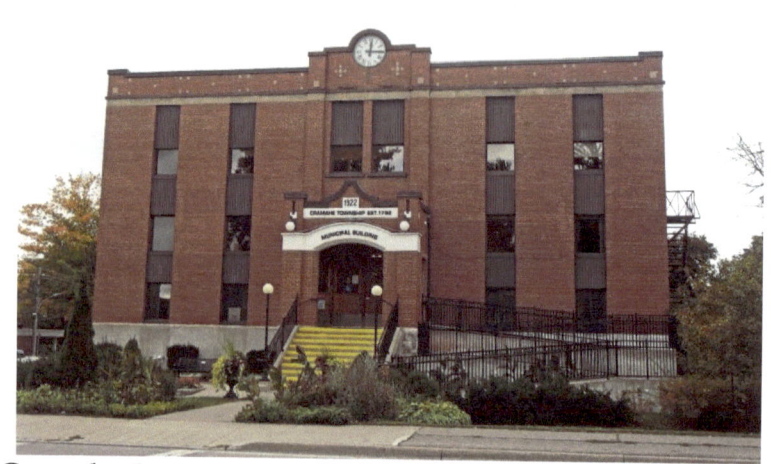
Cramahe Township Municipal Building – 1922 – stepped parapet with clock

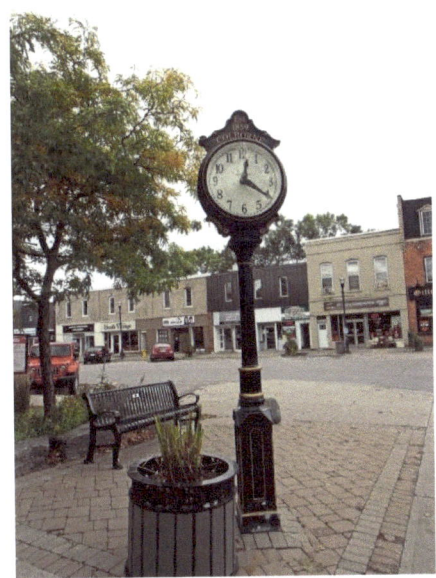

Town Clock

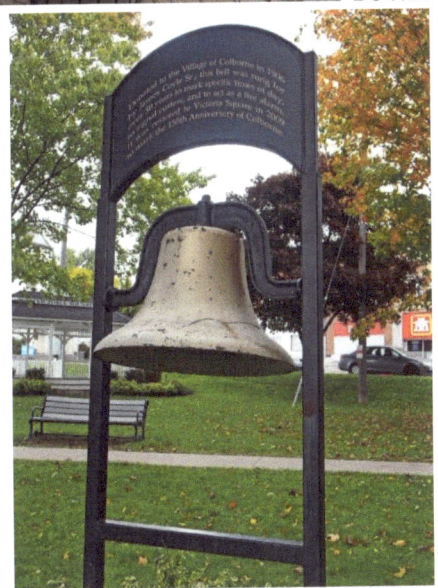

This bell was donated to the Village of Colborne in 1906 by James Coyle Sr. It was rung for over fifty years to mark specific times of day, to signal curfew, and to act as a fire alarm. It was restored to Victoria Square in 2009 to mark the 150th anniversary of Colborne.

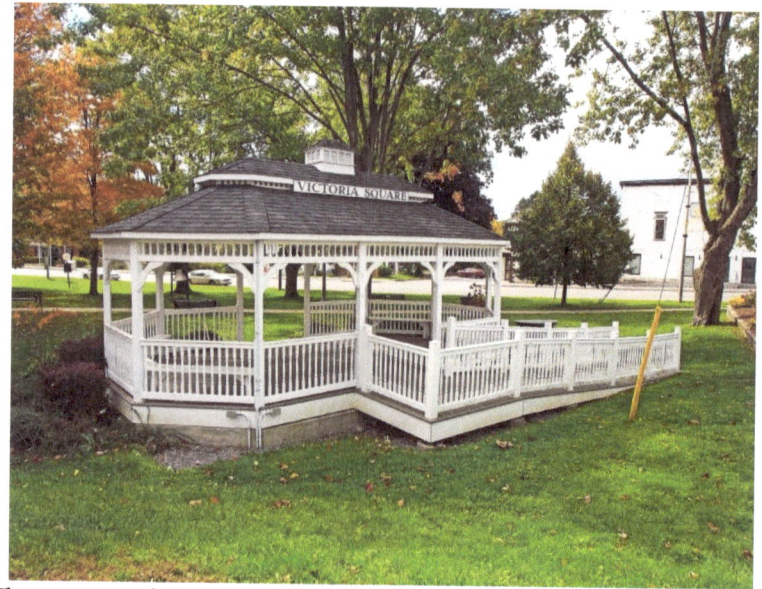

The name of the Square was changed in 1871 to honor the reigning monarch and the settlers' United Empire Loyalist heritage.

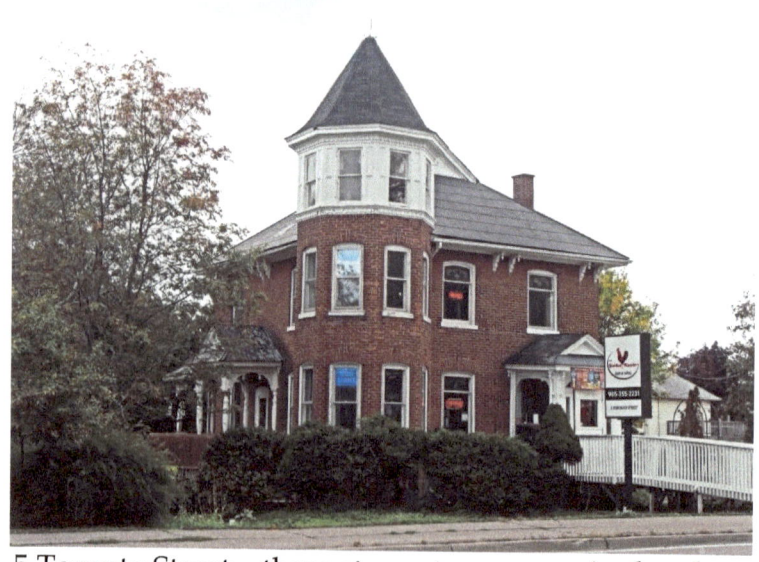

5 Toronto Street – three storey tower, cornice brackets

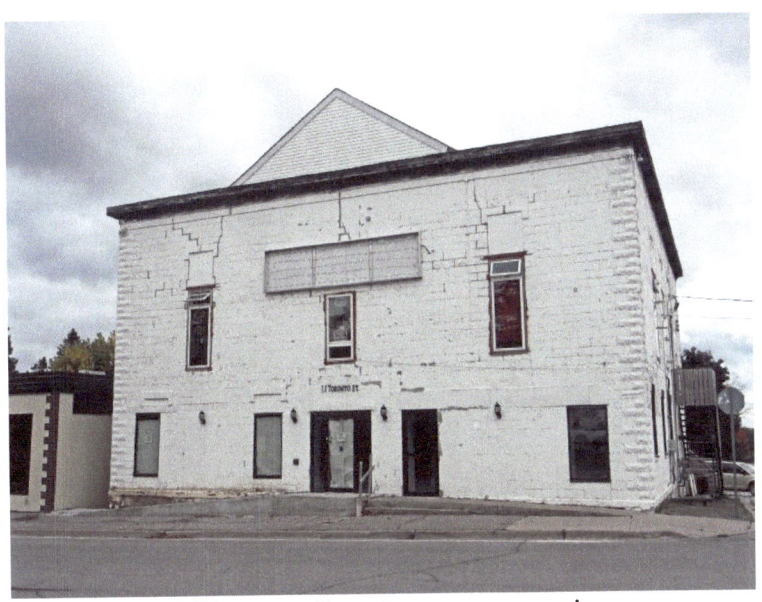

11 Toronto Street – corner quoins

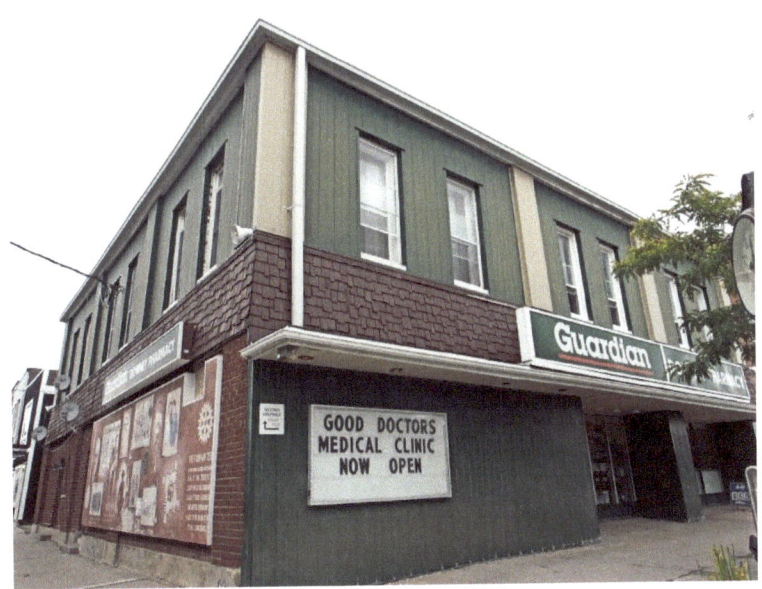

Keeler Block – 1872

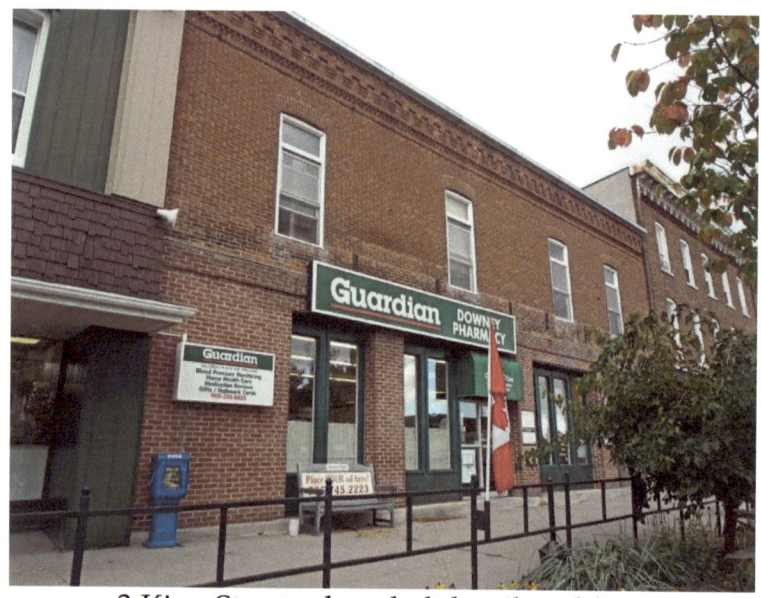

3 King Street – beveled dentil molding

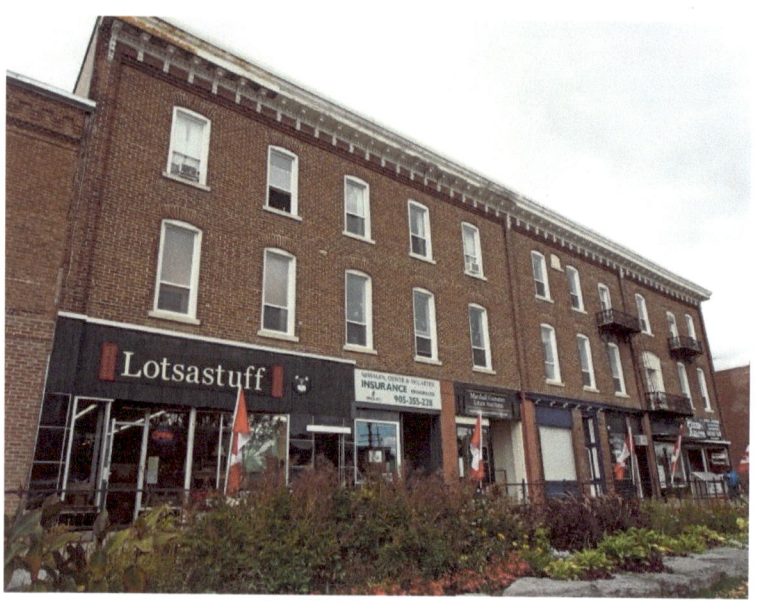

15-29 King Street

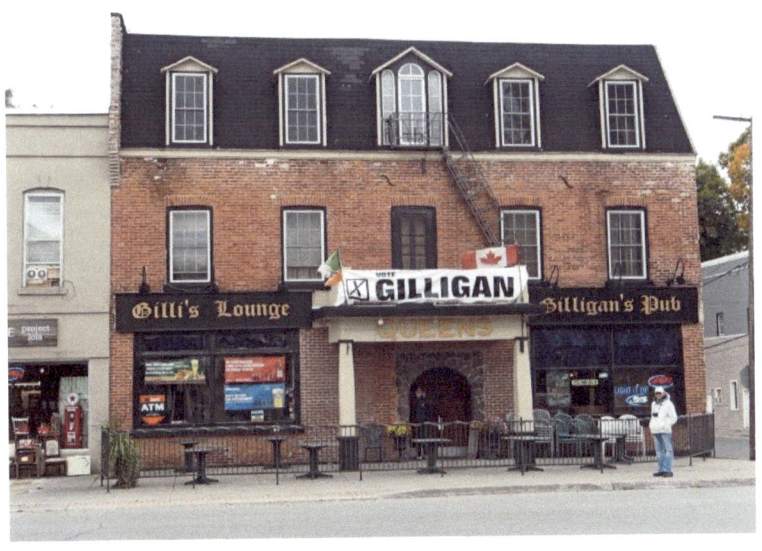

4 King Street – Queen's Hotel – dormers

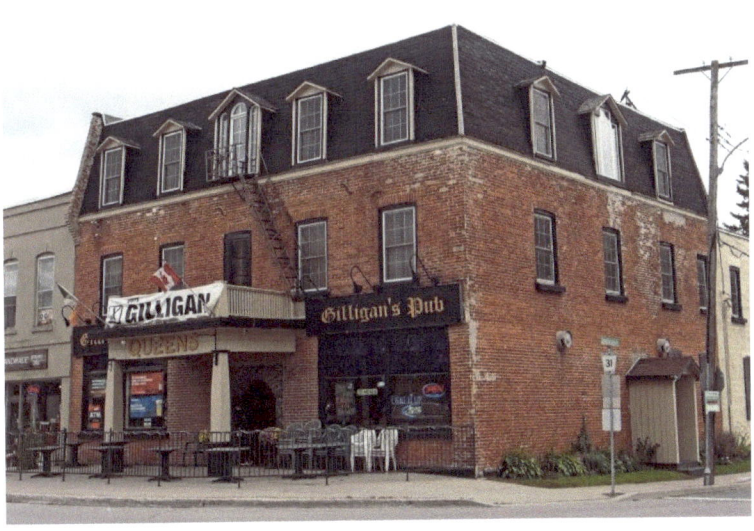

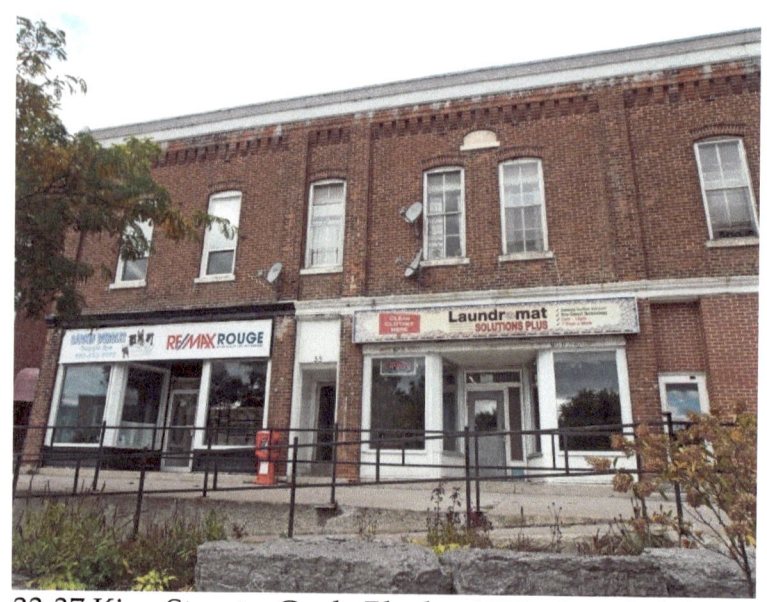

33-37 King Street – Coyle Block – 1839 - beveled dentil molding, pilasters

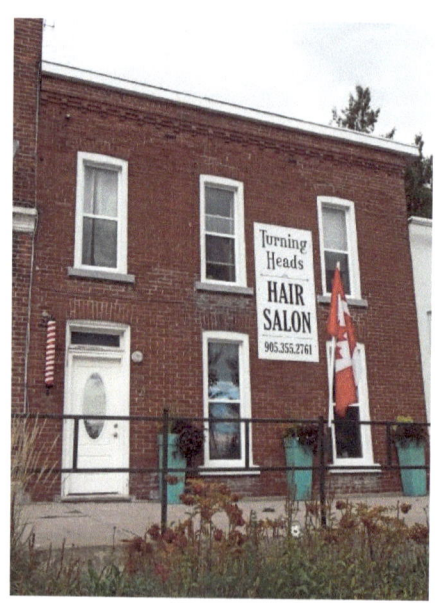

41 King Street

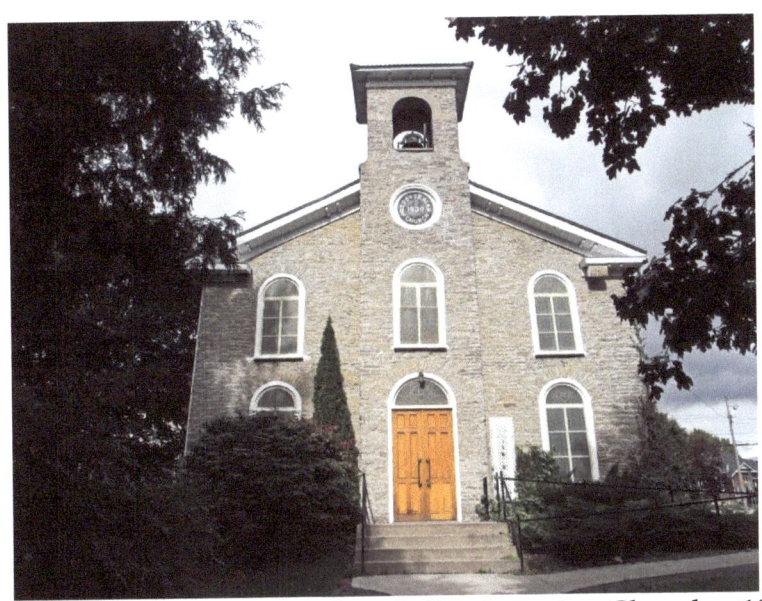

45 King Street – Old St. Andrew's Presbyterian Church – 1830

During the winter of 1829, local limestone was hauled by oxen to this site. The stone church was built in 1830, the pulpit and spire begun in 1832 and completed in 1833. Joseph Abbott Keeler, the town founder and son of the first settler, donated the land to the Presbyterians as he did for the Methodist congregation, though he himself was an Anglican. His only request was that a seat be reserved for him.

The church was designed by Archibald Fraser, a Scottish architect-builder, in a plain and classically proportioned Georgian style.

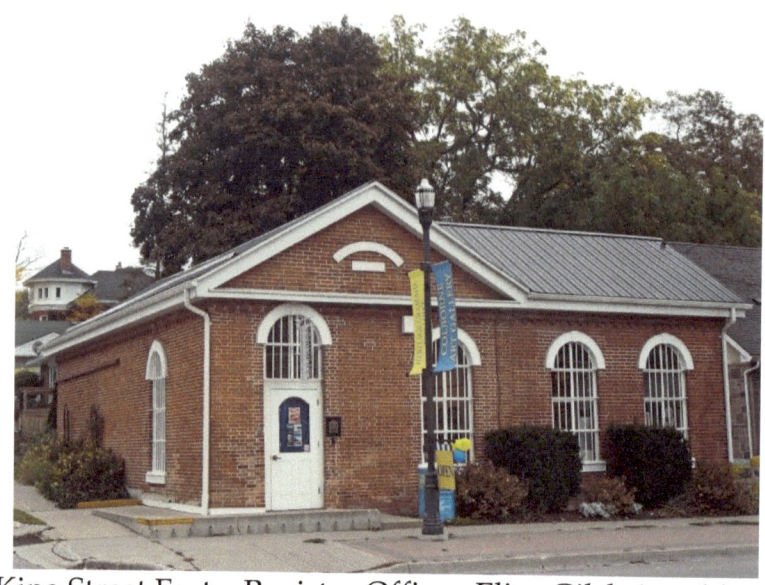

51 King Street East – Registry Office - Eliza Gilchrist, eldest daughter of J.A. Keeler, sold lot 167 to the County of Northumberland and Durham in 1861 for $100.00, for the express purpose of building a County Registry Office. It served that purpose for the next 132 years. Upon closing, the site was retained by the municipality and it is now the home of the Colborne Art Gallery.

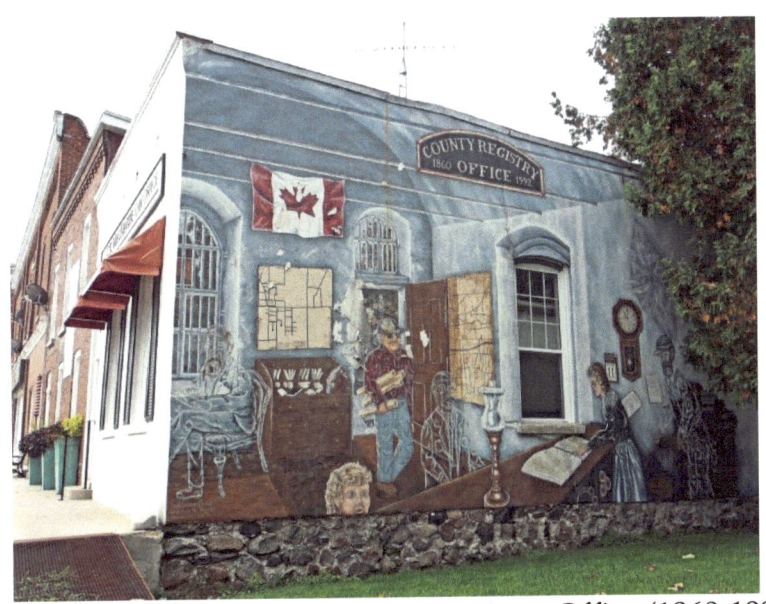

43 King Street – mural of County Registry Office (1860-1992)

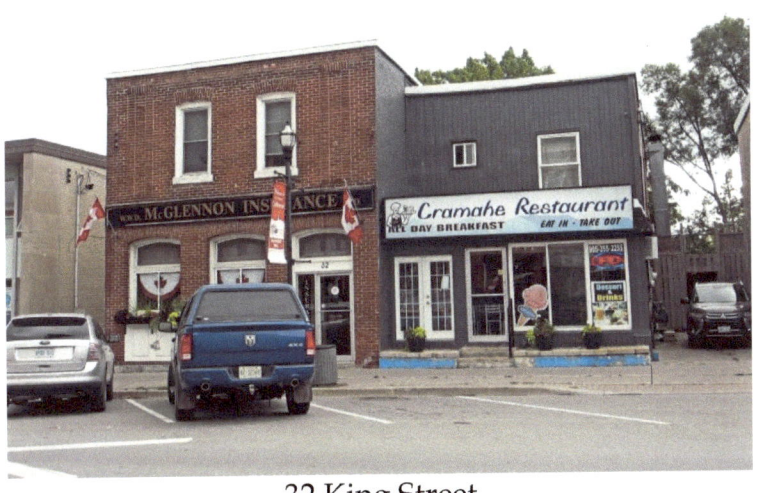

32 King Street

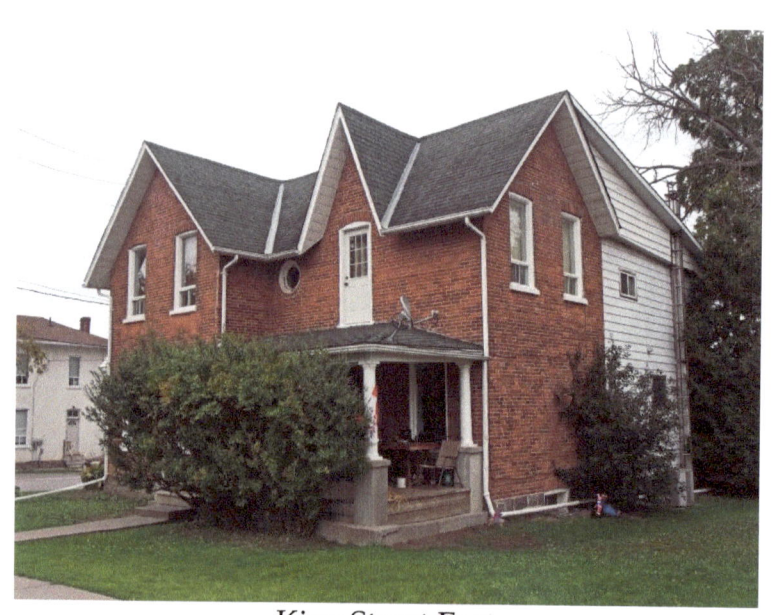

King Street East

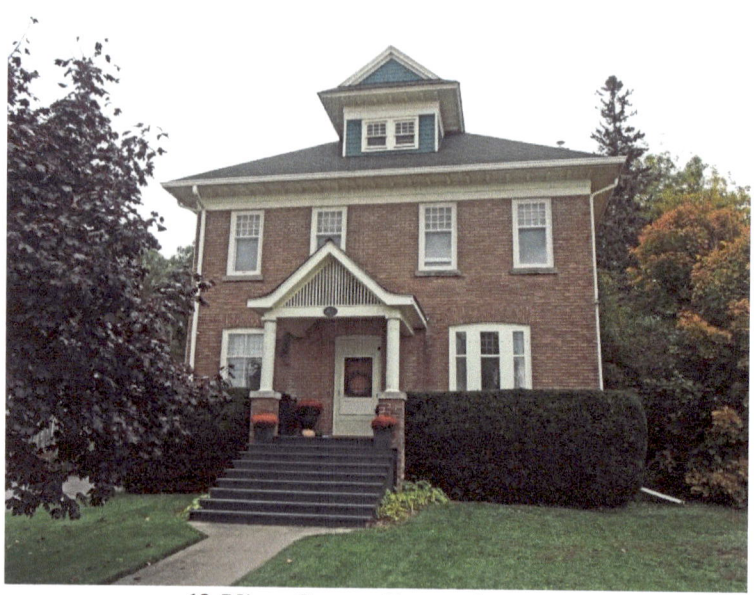

63 King Street East - dormer

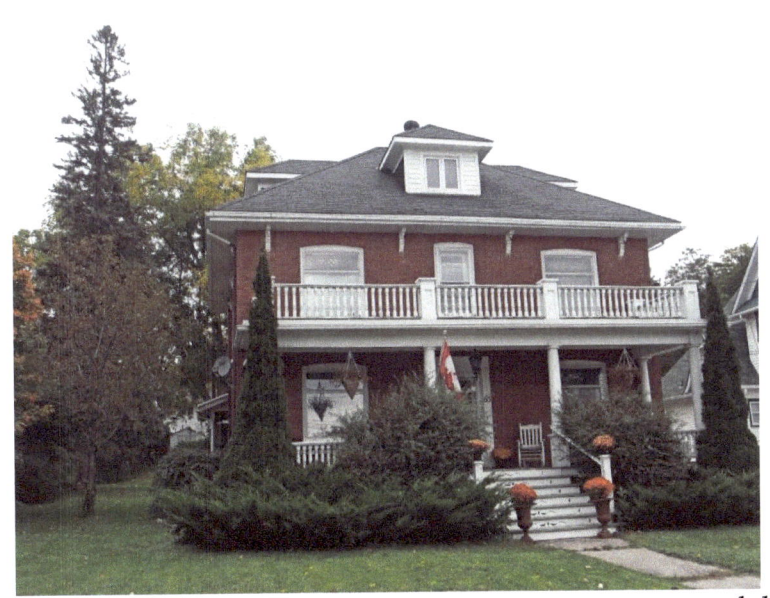

65 King Street East – dormers, two-storey open verandah

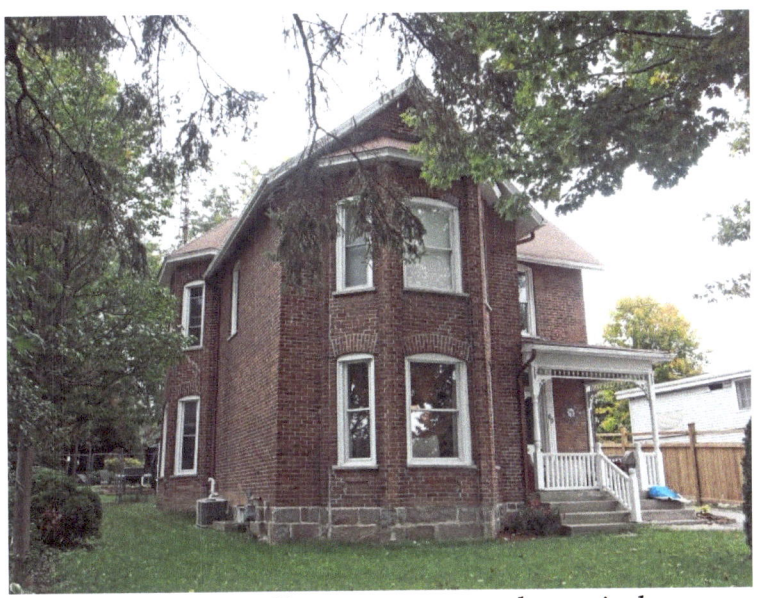

69 King Street East – two-storey bay window

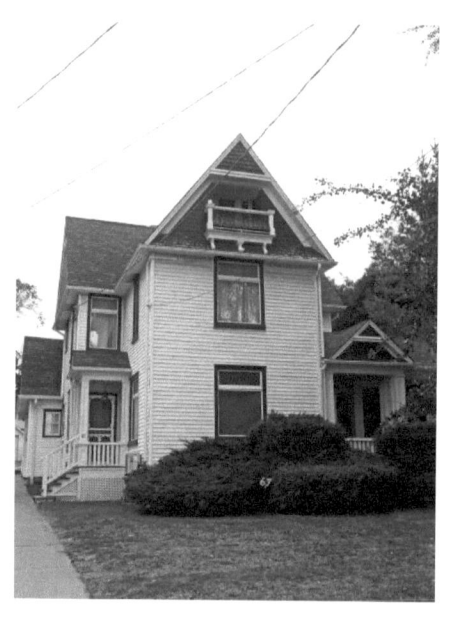

67 King Street East

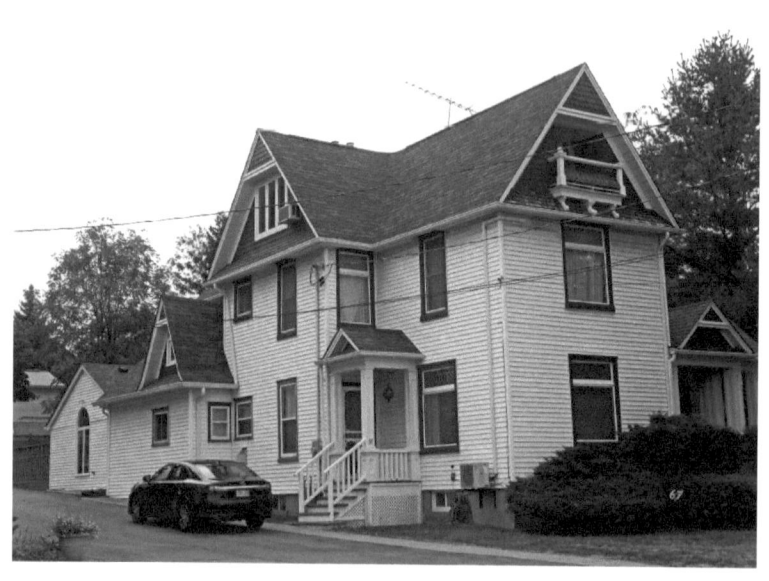

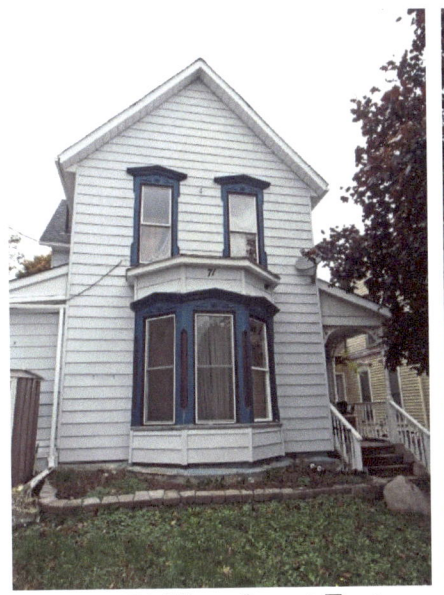 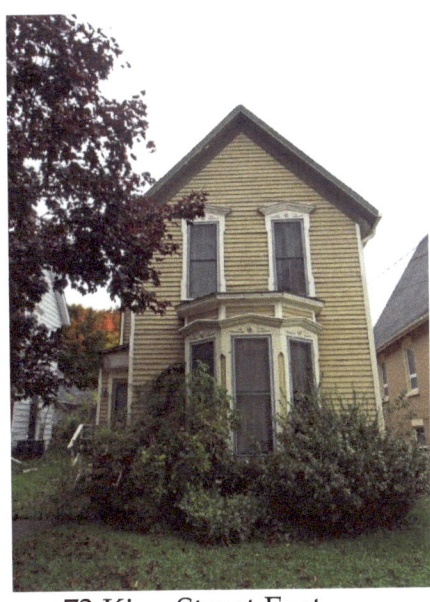

71 King Street East   73 King Street East
bay windows

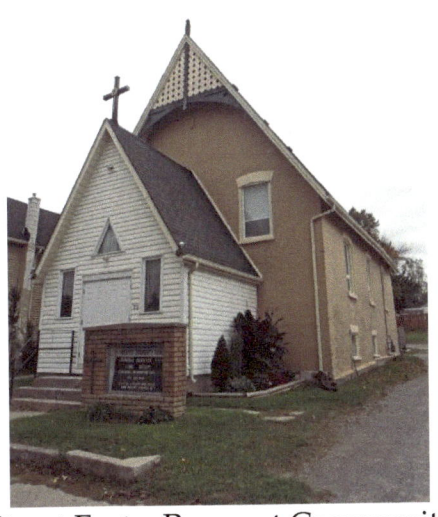

75 King Street East – Prospect Community Church

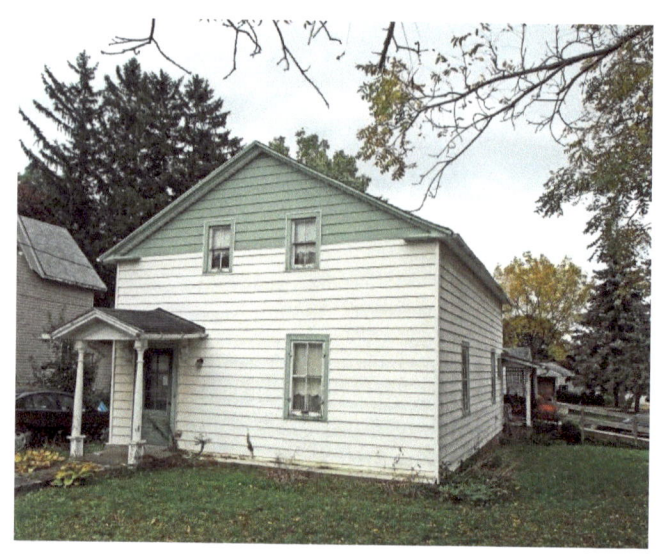

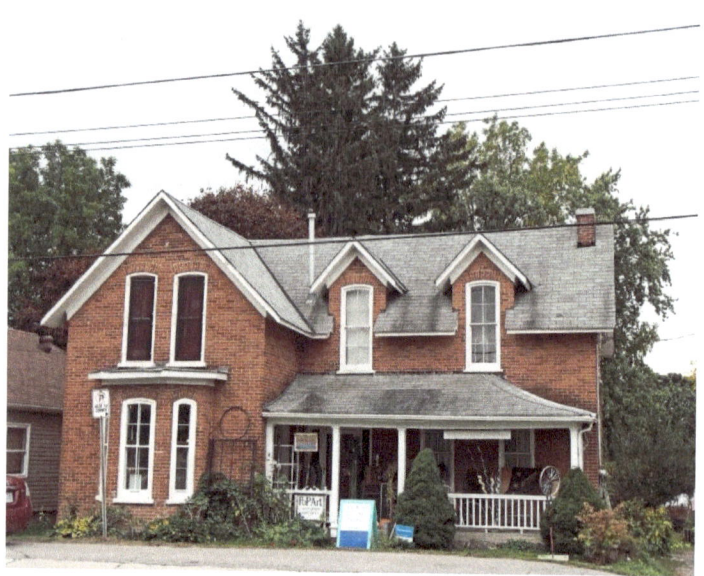

King Street East

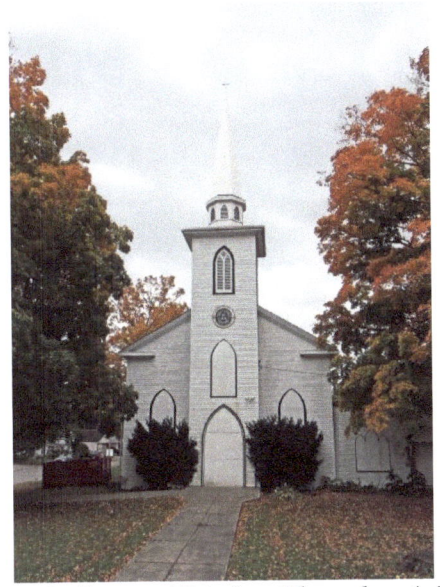

King Street East, Colborne Trinity Church - A.D. 1846 - frame construction, rectangular, with a square tower topped by a short steeple. The chancel was added some years after the main building was erected and the grey-brick parish hall was added in 1910. Trinity is noted for its seven beautiful stained-glass windows. There is a stenciled Gothic window above the main door.

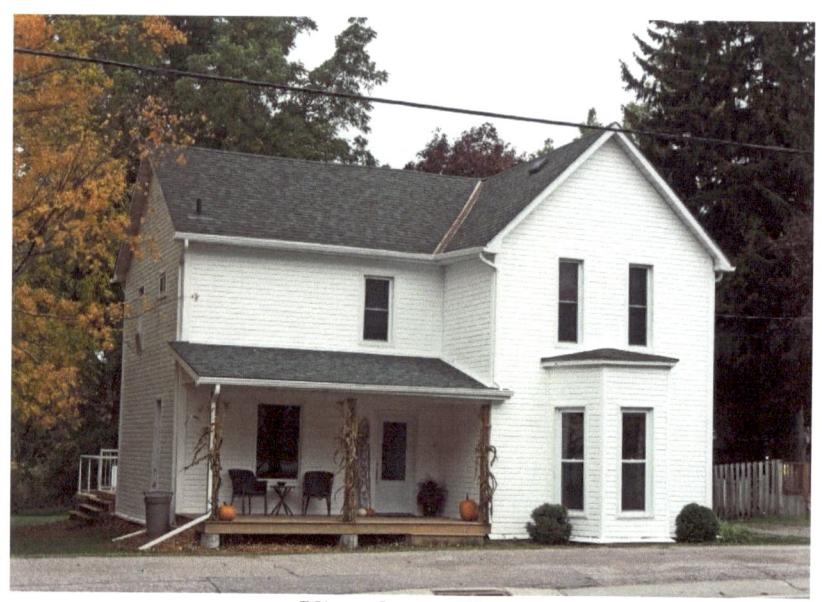

King Street East

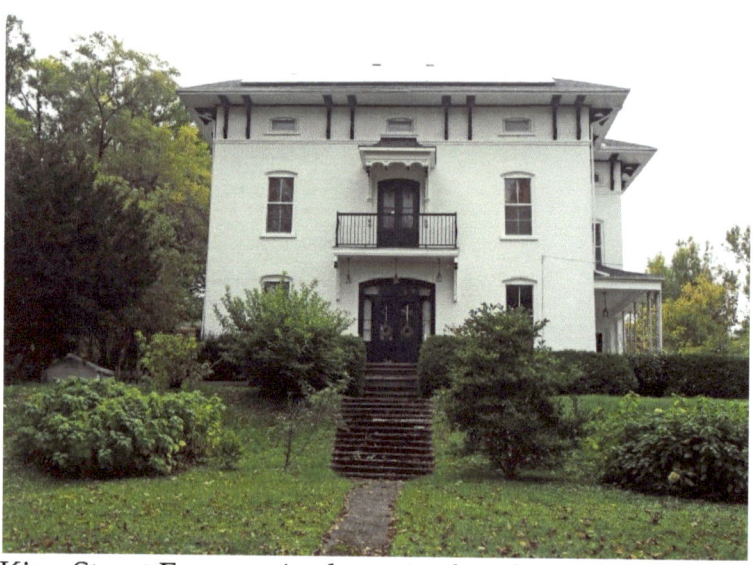

King Street East – paired cornice brackets, second floor balcony, sidelights and transom on front entrance

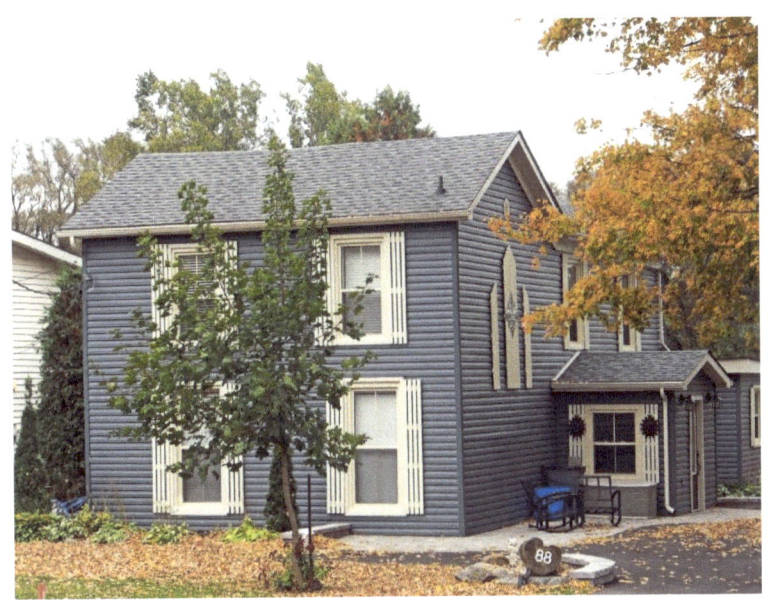

88 King Street East

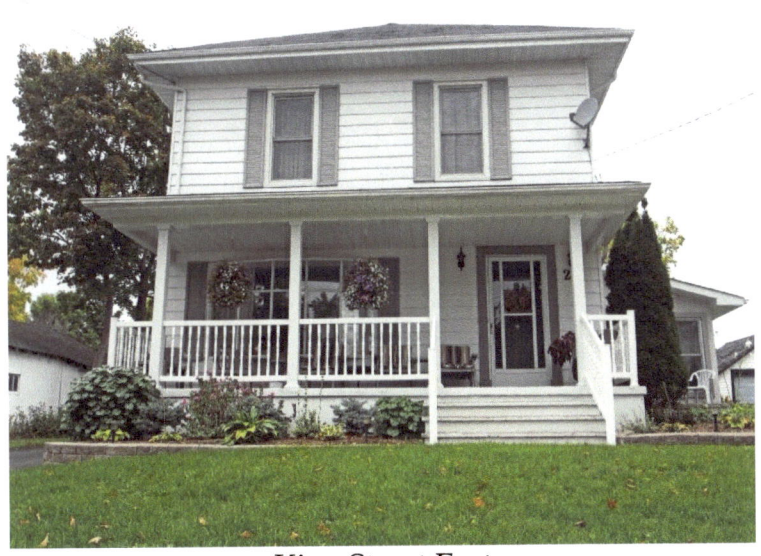

King Street East

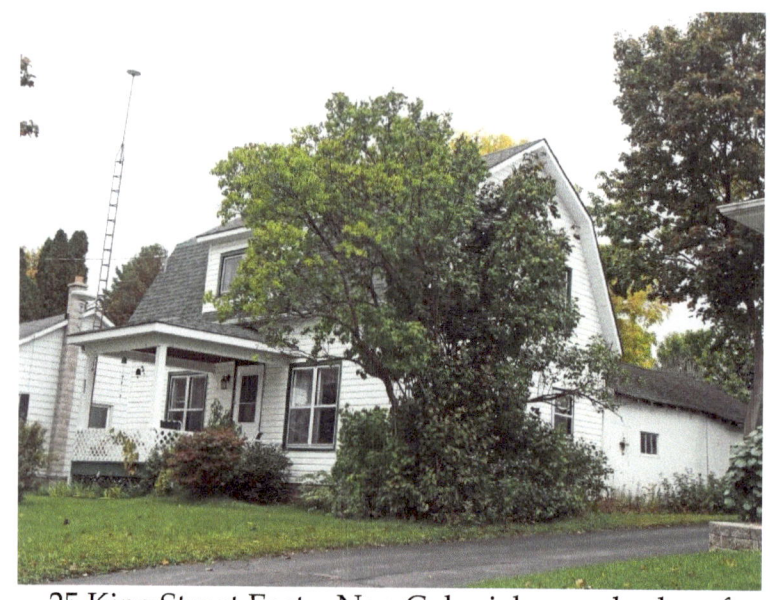

25 King Street East – Neo-Colonial – gambrel roof

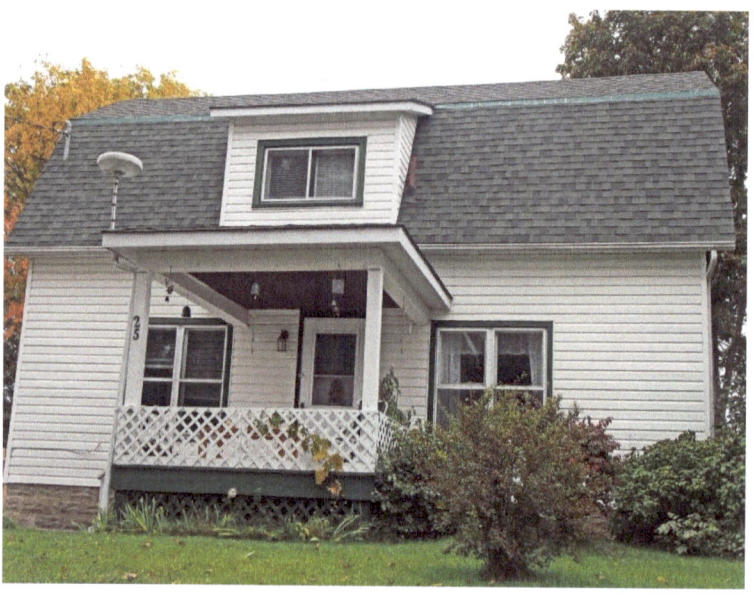

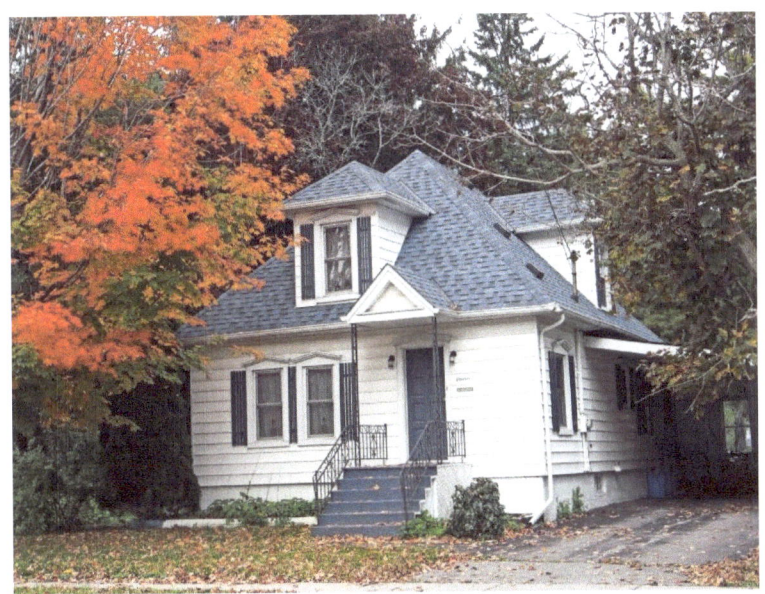

11 Church Street East

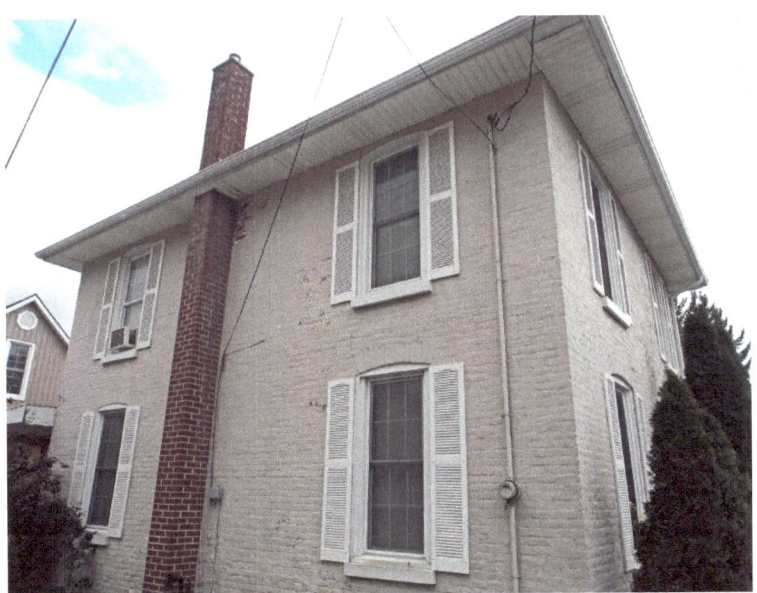

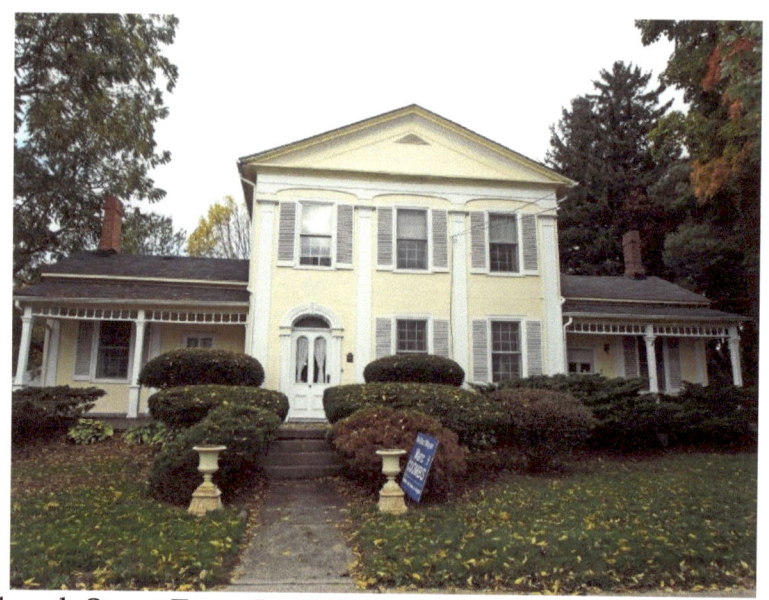

9 Church Street East - In 1820, Joseph Abbott Keeler built this beautiful Neo-Classical house.

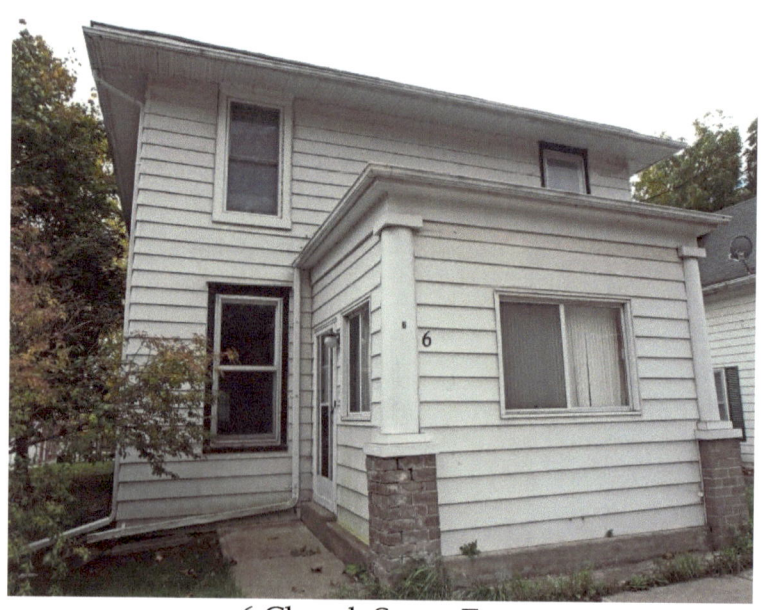

6 Church Street East

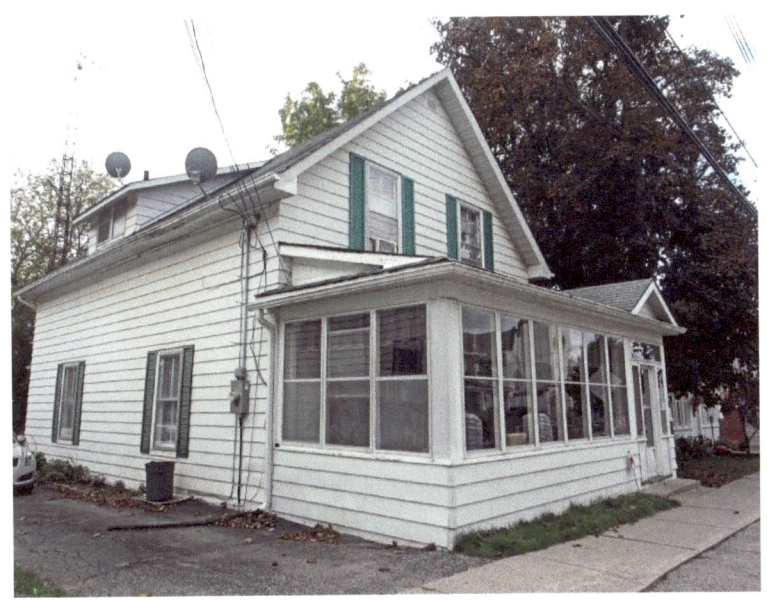

Church Street East

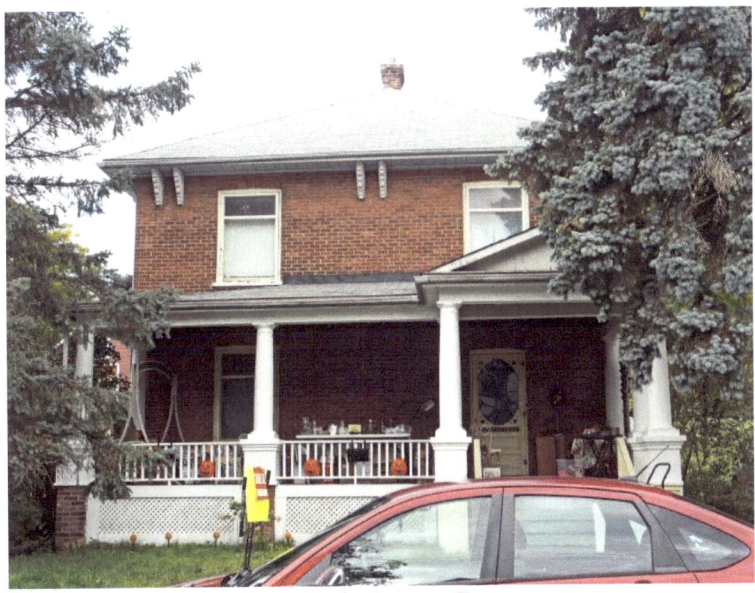

Church Street East

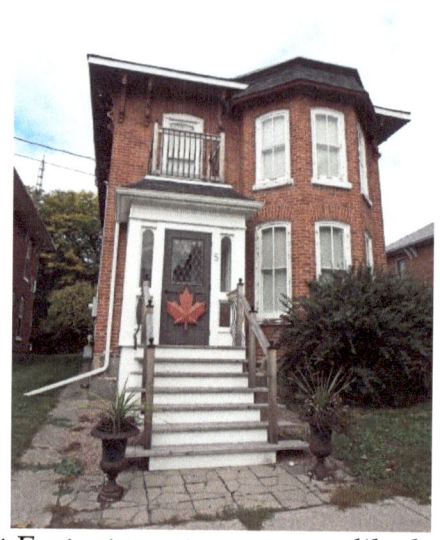

5 Church Street East – two-storey tower-like bay, second floor balcony

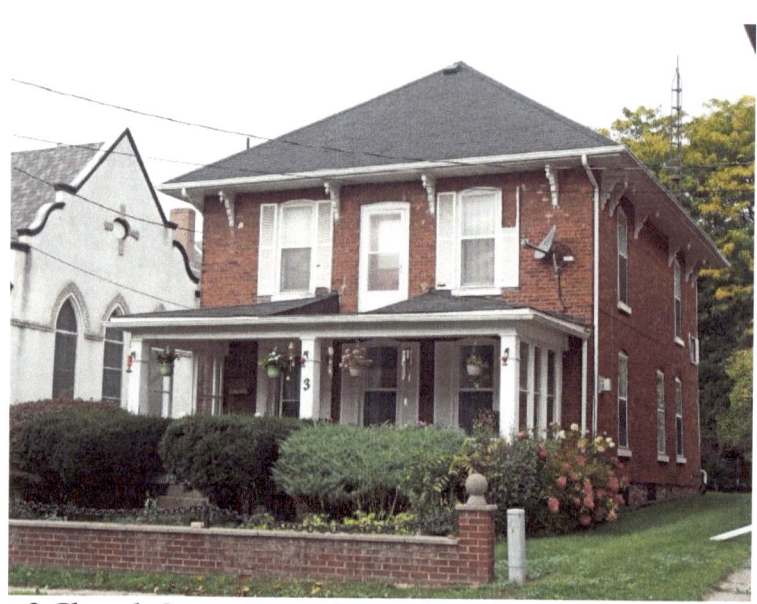

3 Church Street East – hipped roof, cornice brackets

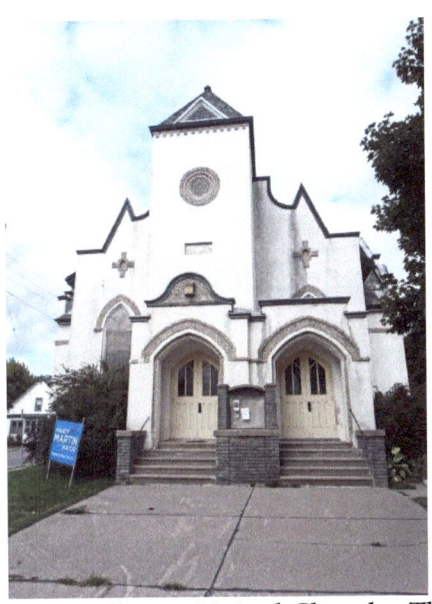

1 Church Street East – Colborne United Church - The church as it appears today was built in 1862. Its imposing Gothic Revival features include angular-shaped gables, a high pitch double cross gable roof, and a pyramidal dormer front tower with lancet windows. The Daniel Lewis Simmons family donated the pipe organ to the church in 1910.

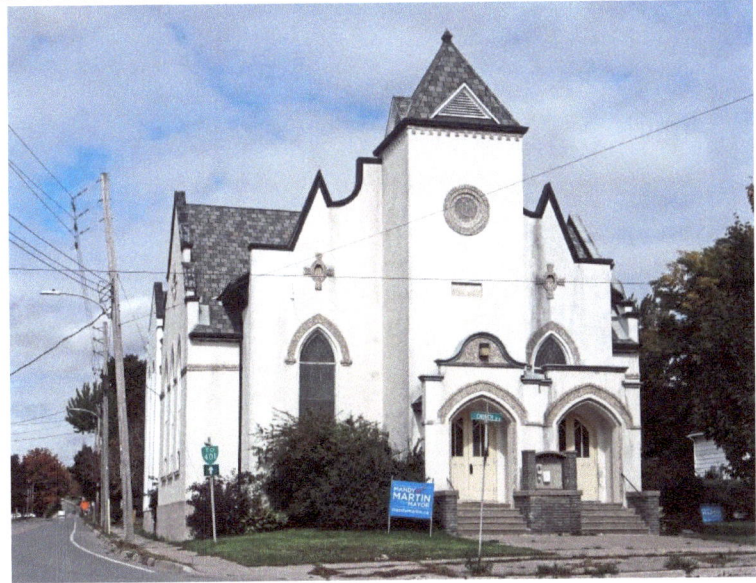

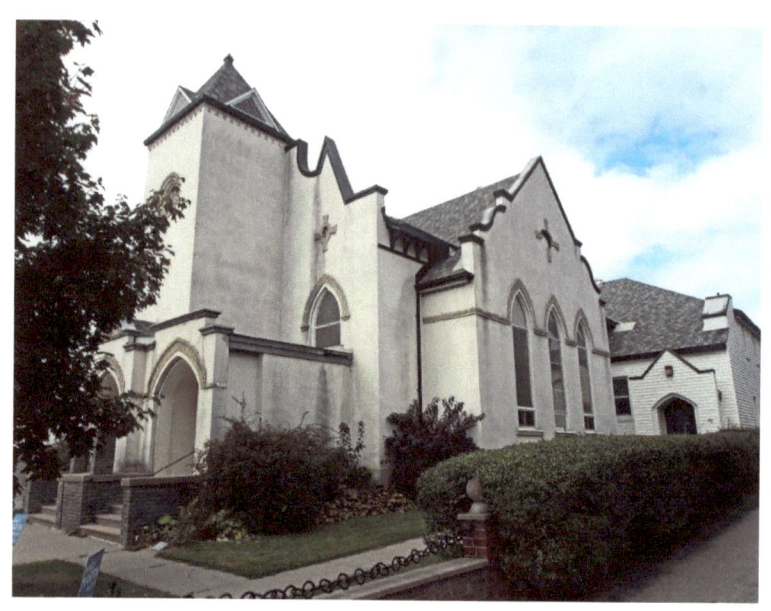

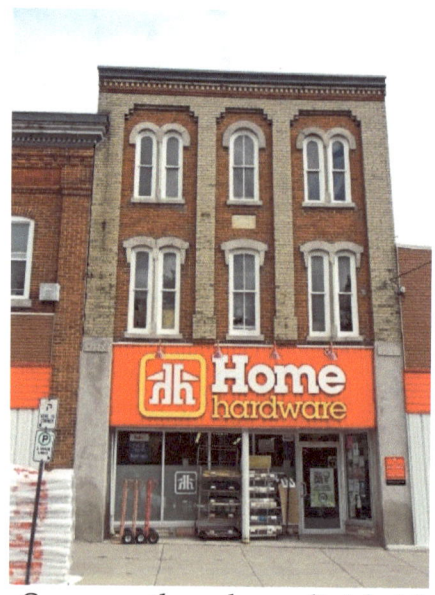

24 Victoria Square – three bays divided by pilasters

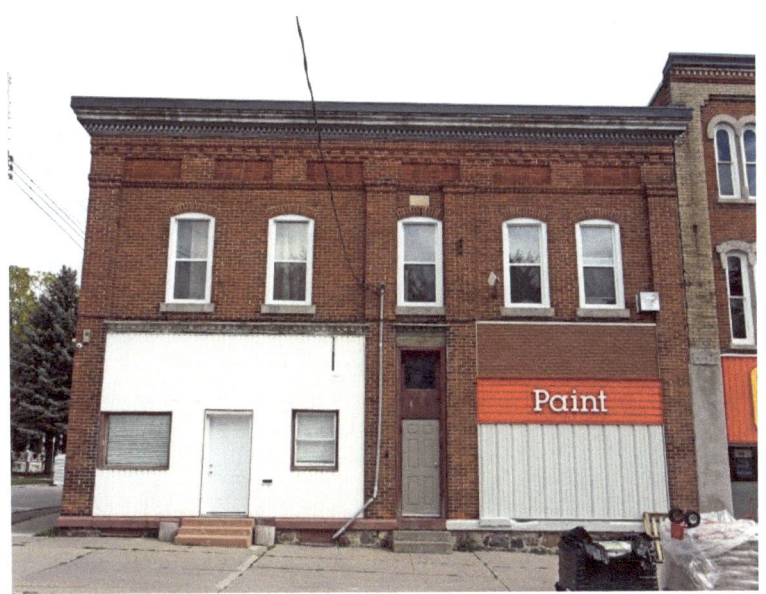

Victoria Square

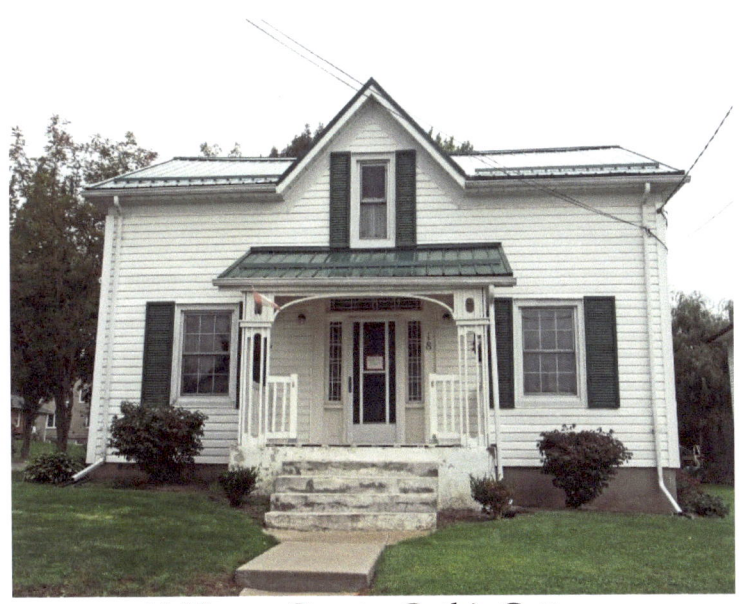

18 Victory Street – Gothic Cottage

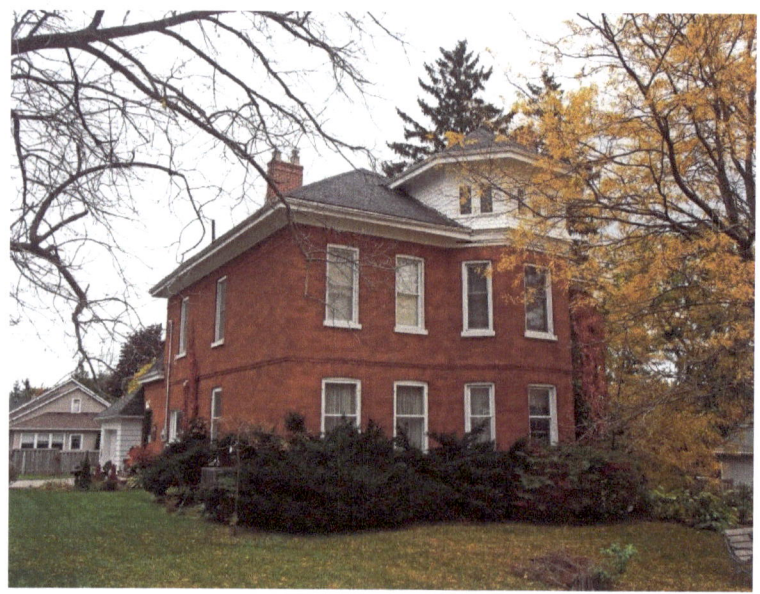

8 Victory Street - During the reign of Queen Anne (1702-1714) an architectural style was born and it enjoyed a revival, particularly in the New World, in the latter part of the 19th century. 8 Victory Lane (as it was then known) is a fine example of this style of architecture. It is characterized by fine brickwork in warm, soft finished tones, terracotta panels and crisply painted white woodwork.

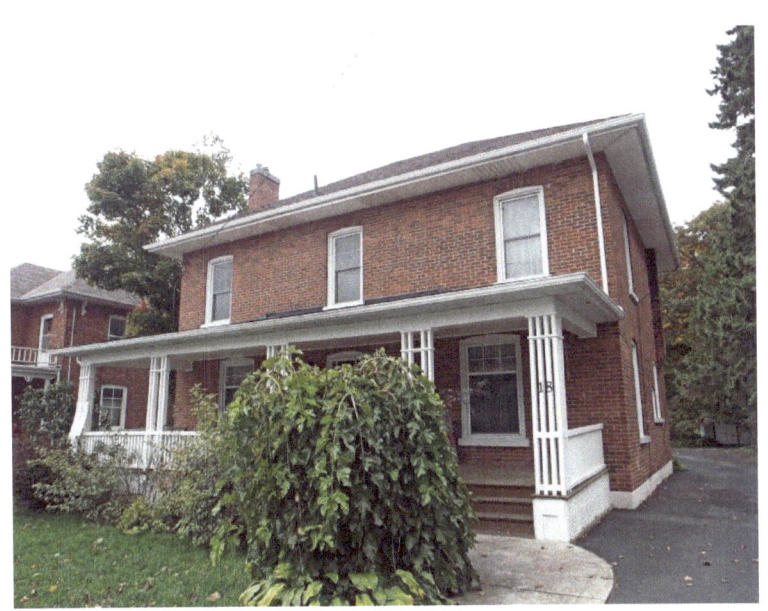

18 Burnham Avenue

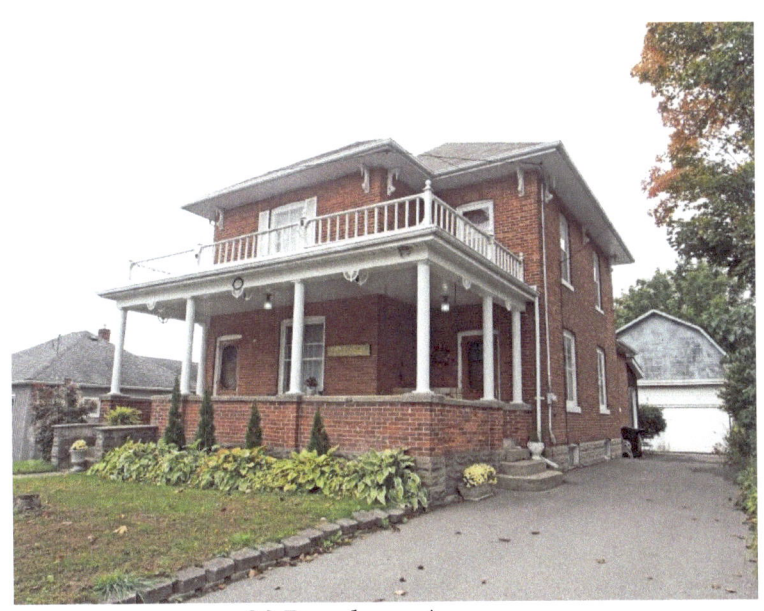

20 Burnham Avenue

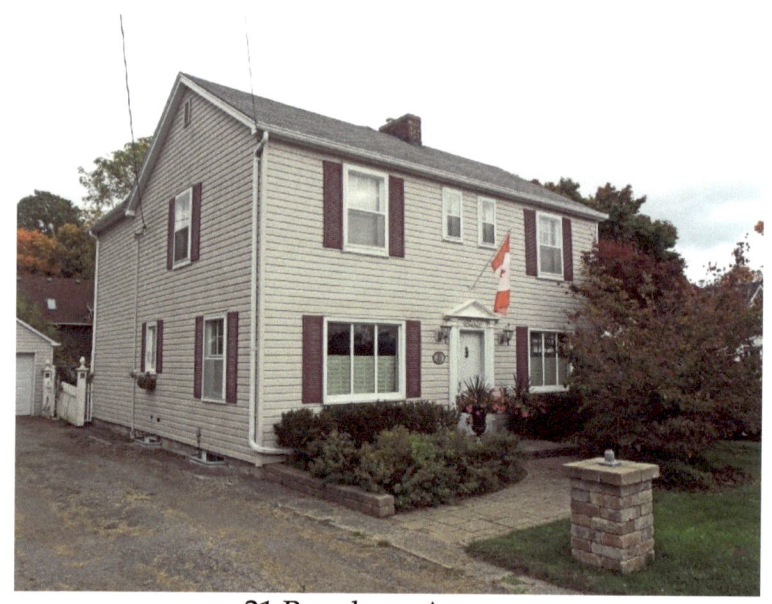

21 Burnham Avenue

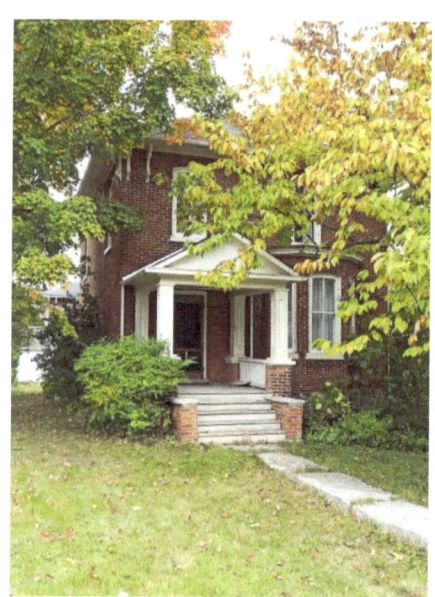

25 Division Street

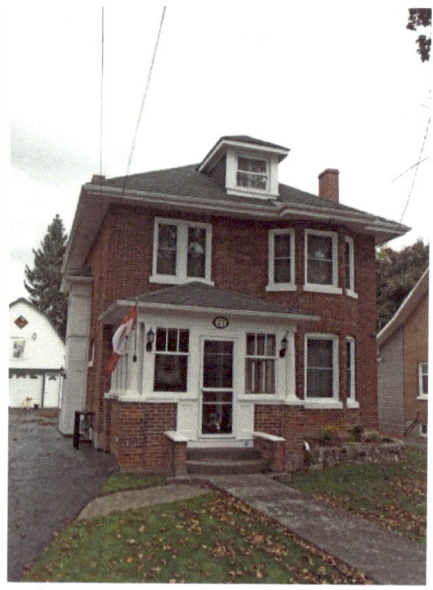

27 Division Street

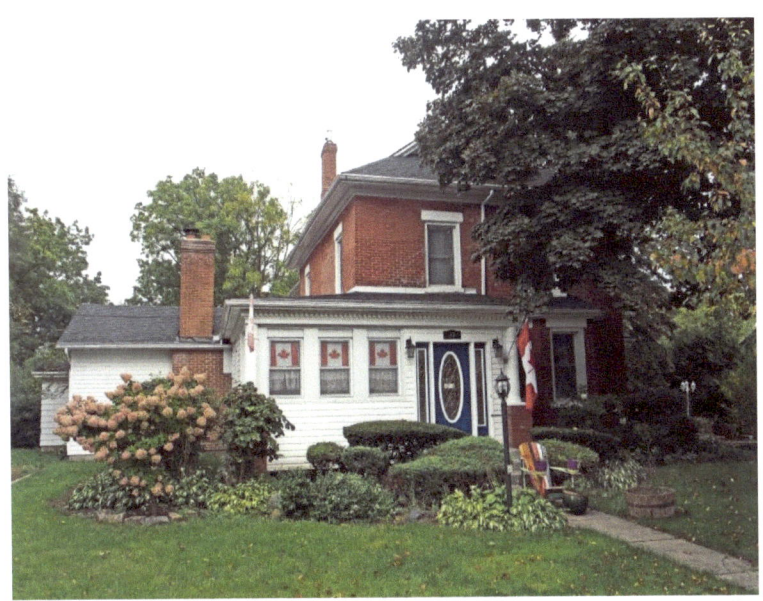

17 Division Street has always been "The Doctors' House" over its long life, beginning in 1888 with Dr. Richard Thorburn. In 1906 Dr. Thomas Bruce Hewson acquired the property and in 1911 he sold to Dr. James Archer Brown.

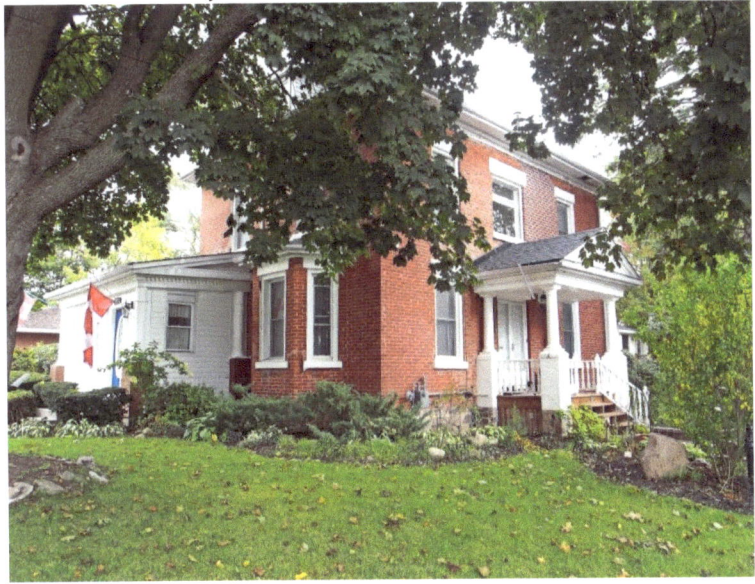

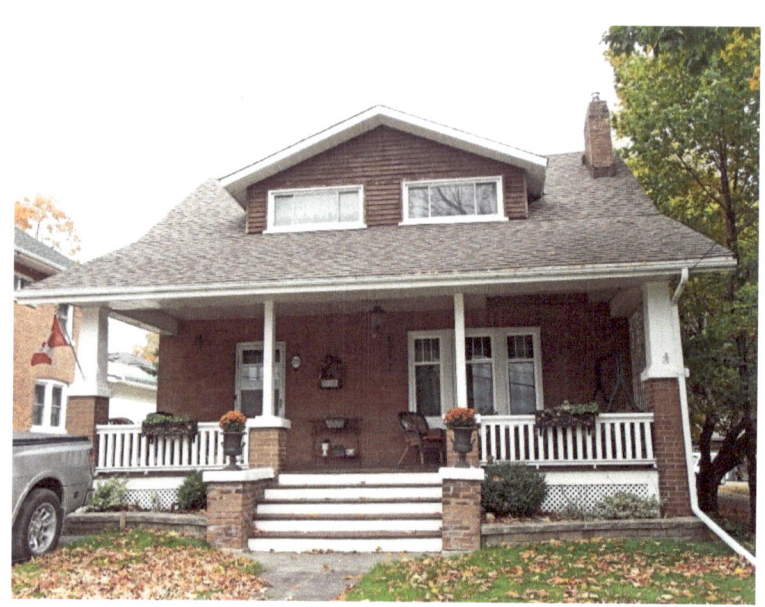

29 Division Street

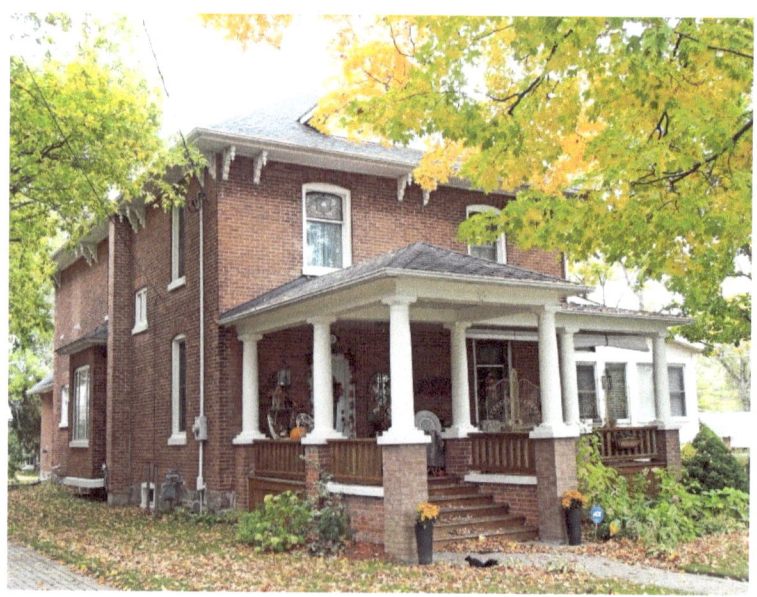

33 Division Street

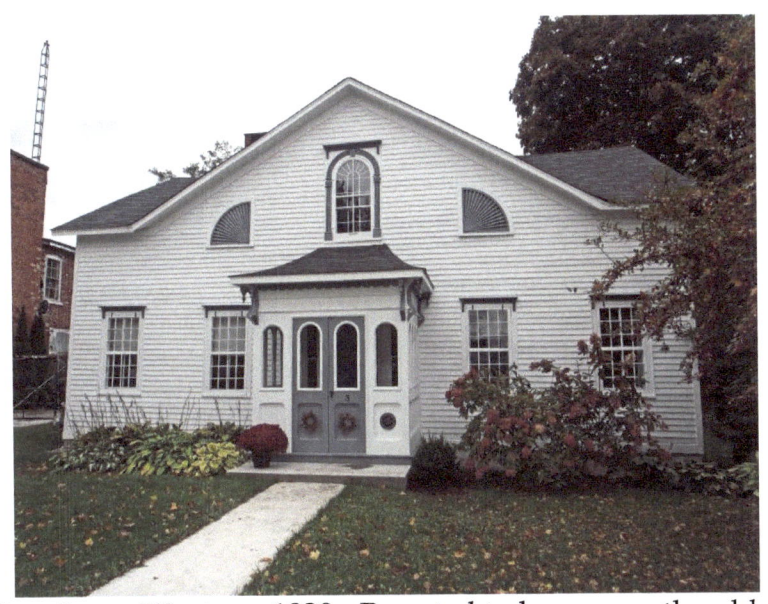

3 King Street West – c. 1820 - Reputed to be among the oldest dwellings in Colborne, this was the home of Scottish immigrant John Steele and his wife Mary Spalding from 1831-1843. However there is reason to believe the house predates 1820. Steele, a founder of Queen's University held many other posts such as magistrate, newspaper editor, Board of Education trustee, member of literacy and agricultural societies etc. In 1843, the Steeles moved to Grafton and sold 3 King Street West to Cuthbert Cumming, a Hudson's Bay trader. He sold it in 1858 to the Scougale family, local dry goods merchants, whose business was in the building next door. The Thorntons, part of the Scougale family, lived here for only nine years of the Scougale clan's 101 year occupancy, yet the house carries their name.

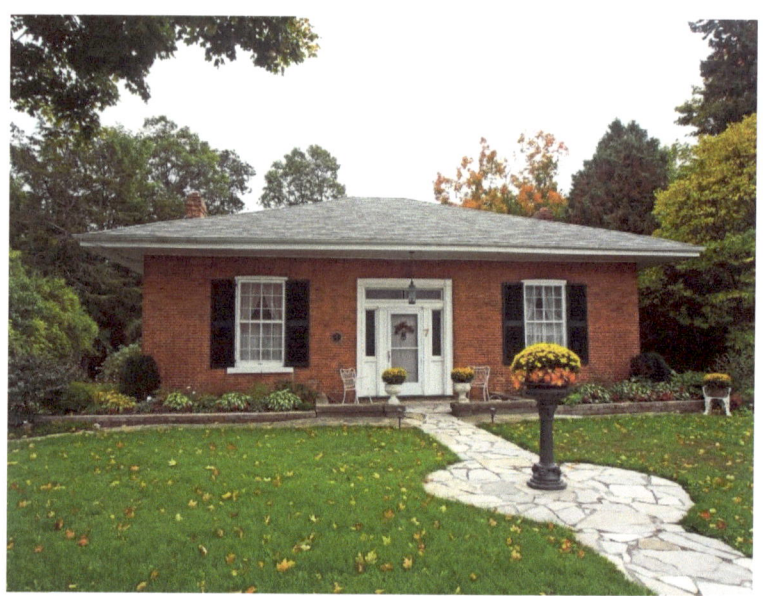

7 King Street West – c. 1830 – In 1846, Cuthbert Cumming and his wife Jane McMurray, acquired a portion of this two acre property, and the balance in 1852. Cumming was born in Scotland and after working in the Canadian west and Quebec, he retired as a Chief Trader for the Hudson Bay Company. He remained in Colborne for many years, listed in the census records as "a gentleman" until his demise in 1870. The front elevation of this classic Regency Cottage with its low profile and deep roof overhang hides a secret. There are actually five levels, including a stone basement that housed the kitchen and servants in the mid-19th century.

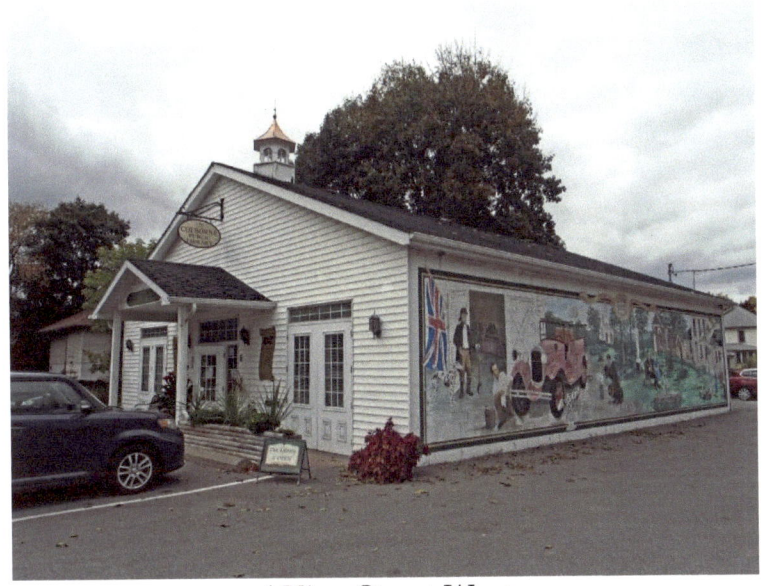

6 King Street West

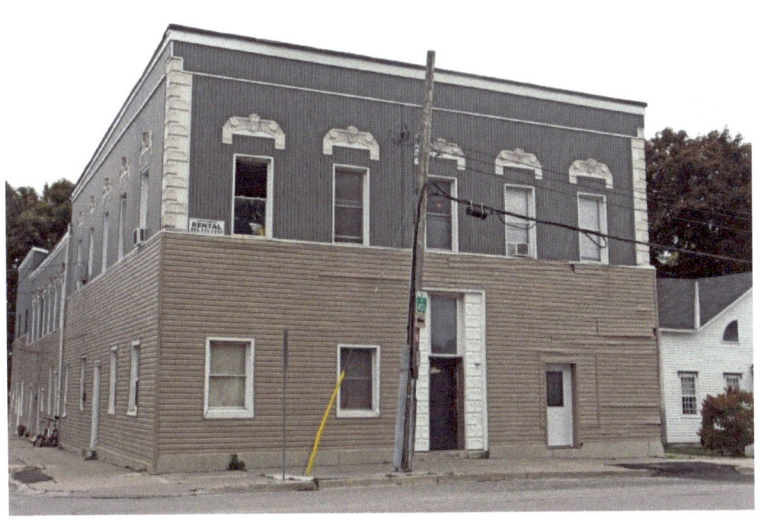

King Street West

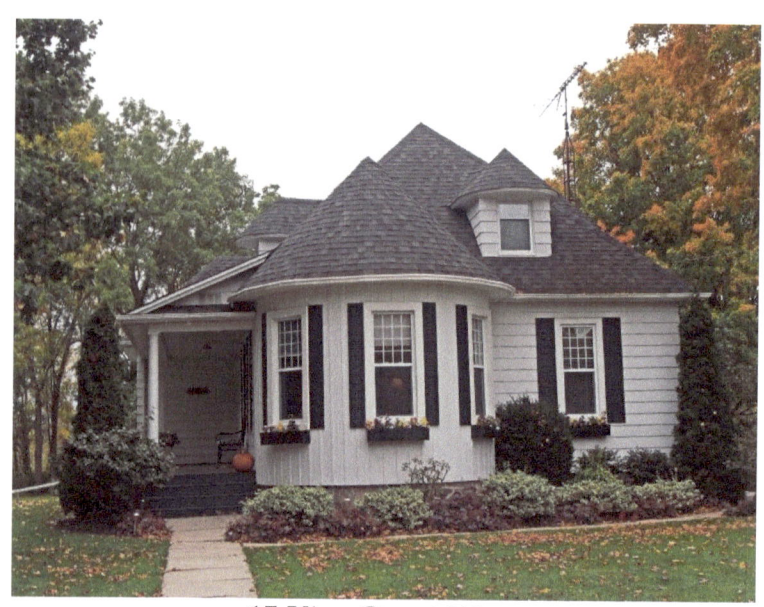

15 King Street West

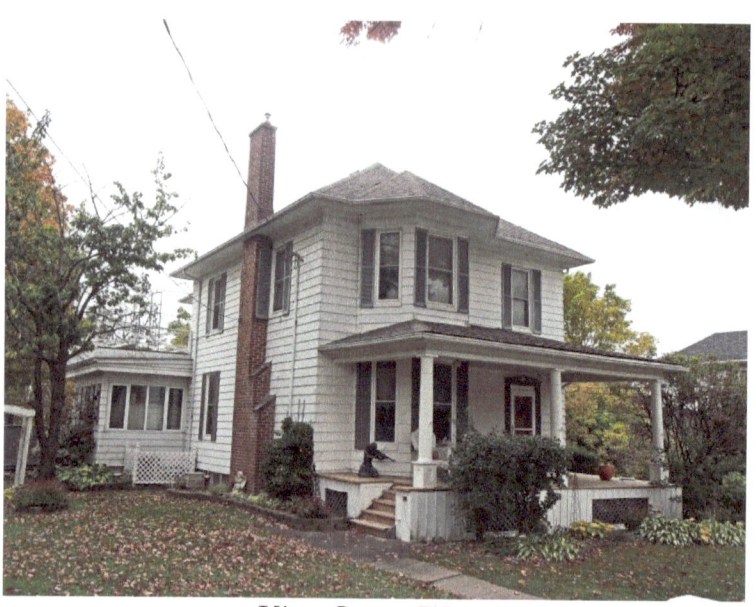

King Street West

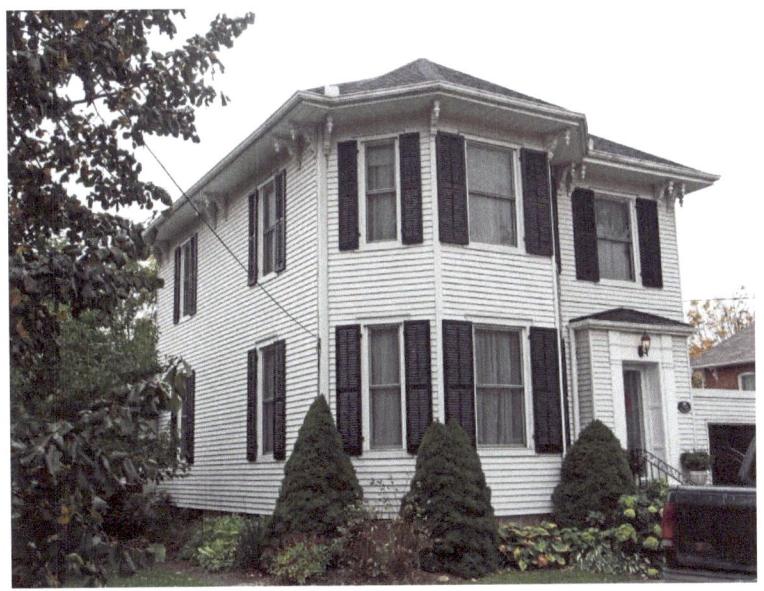

19 King Street West

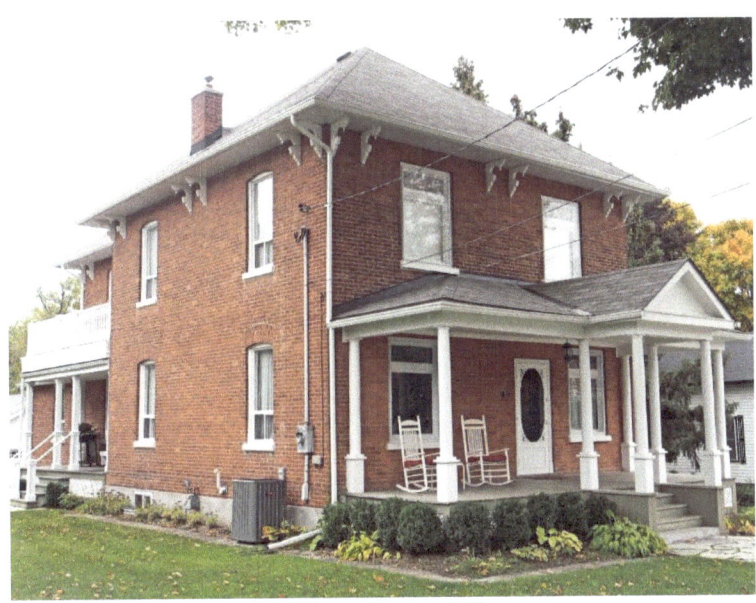

21 King Street West

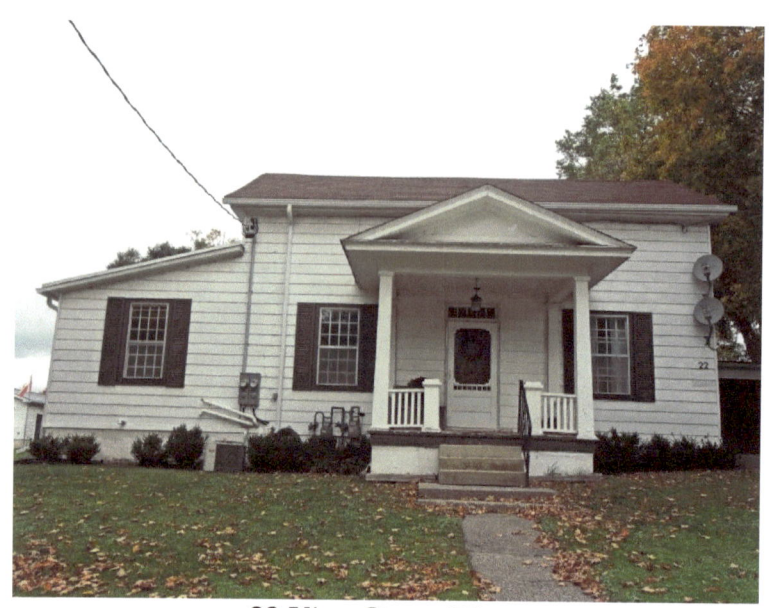

22 King Street West

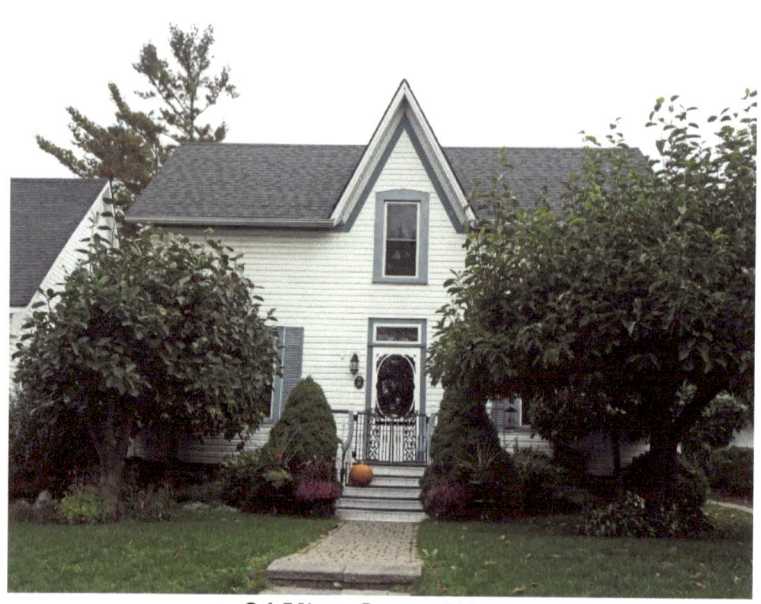

26 King Street West

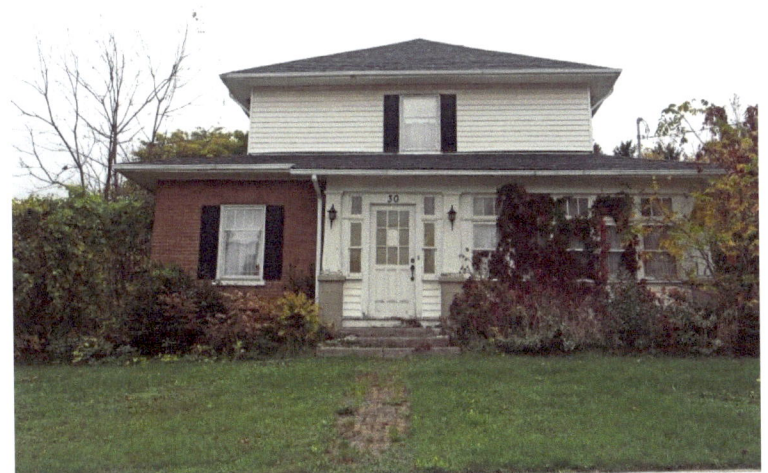

30 King Street West

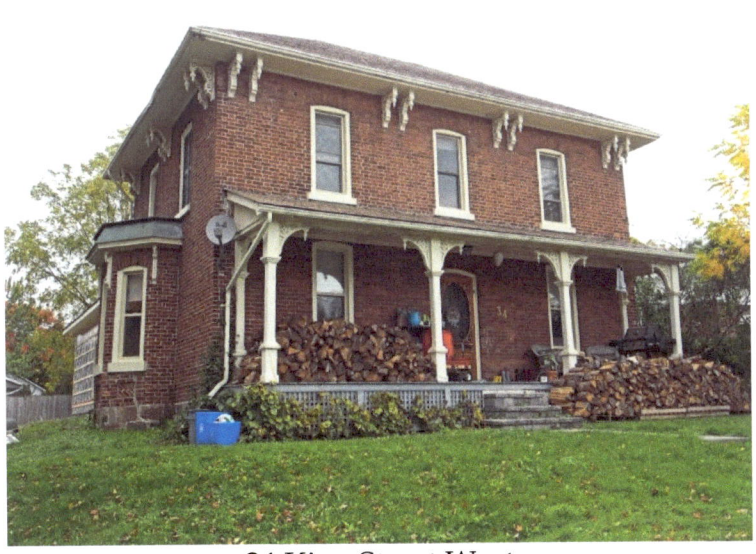

34 King Street West

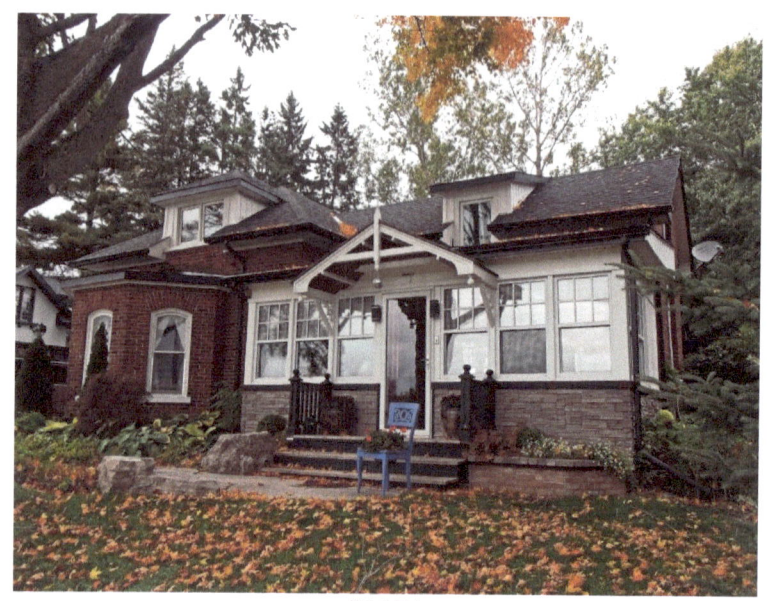

#1151

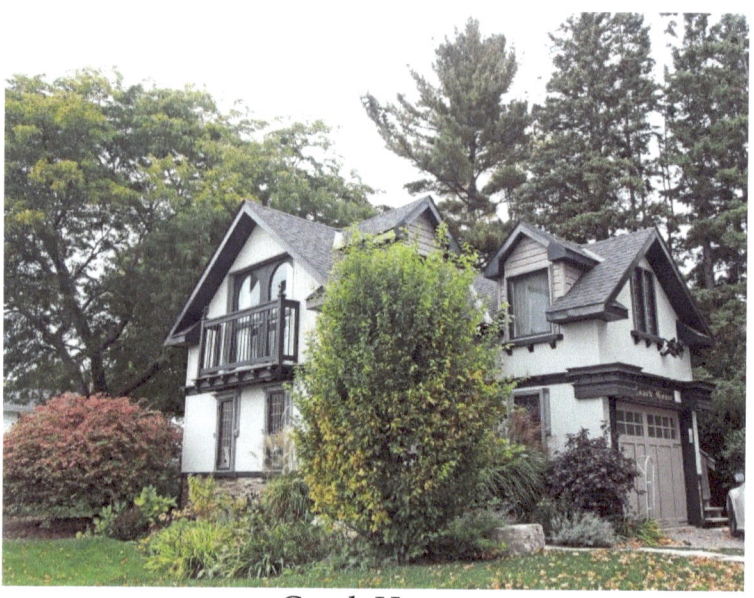

Coach House

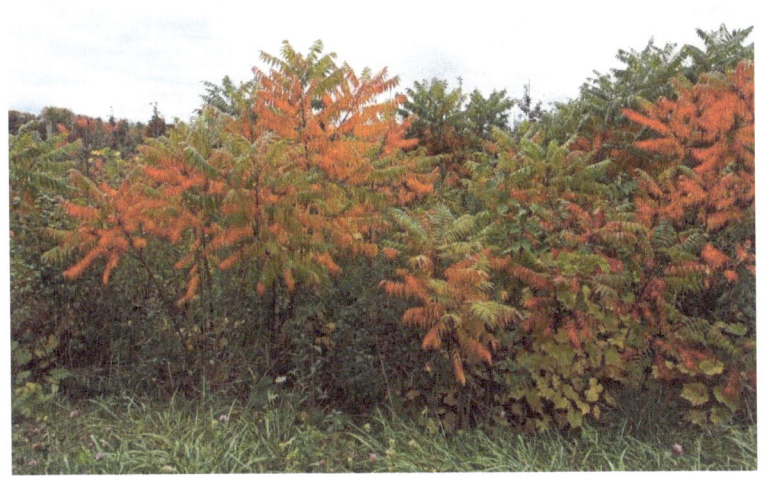

Sumac have turned their green to red

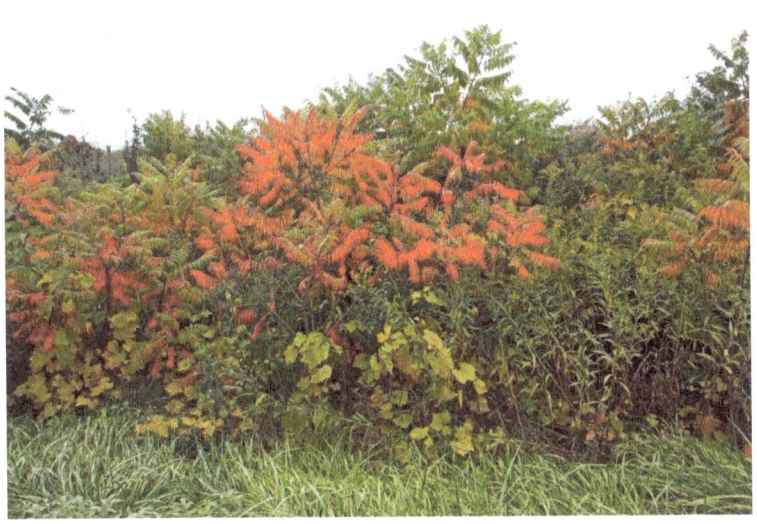

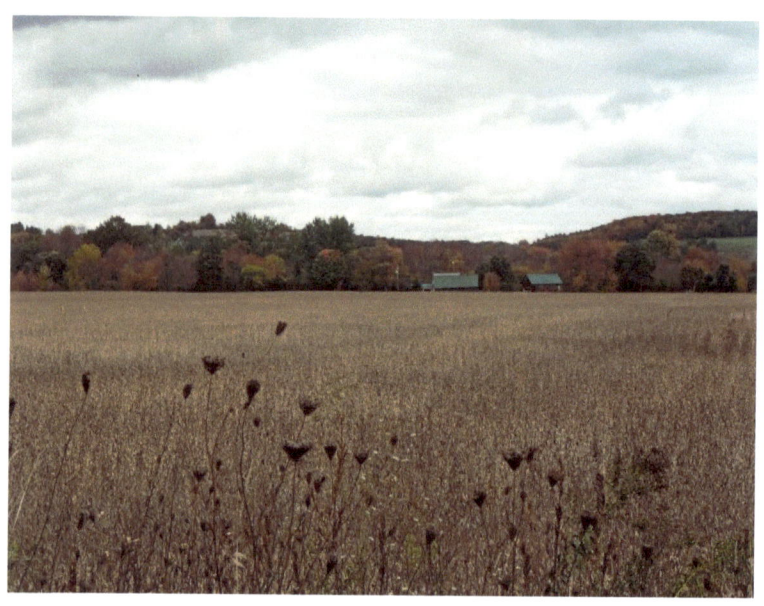

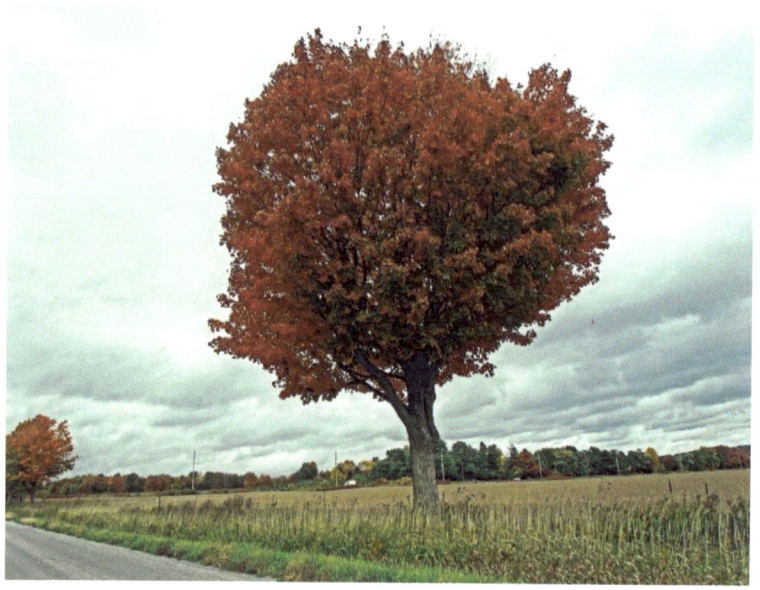

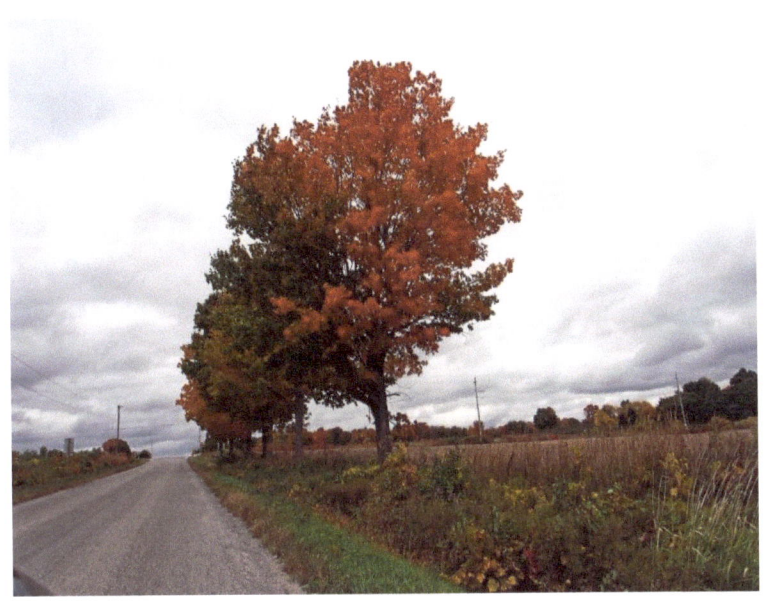

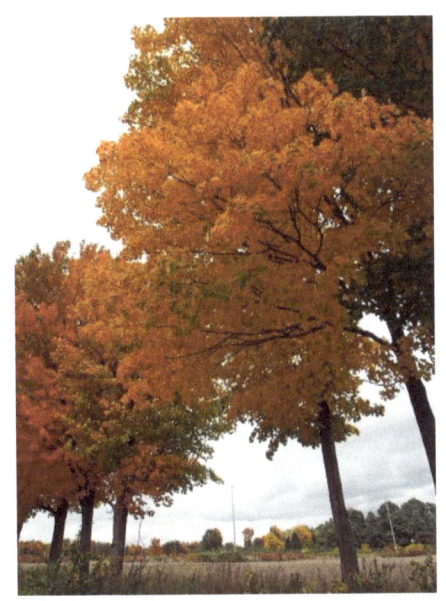

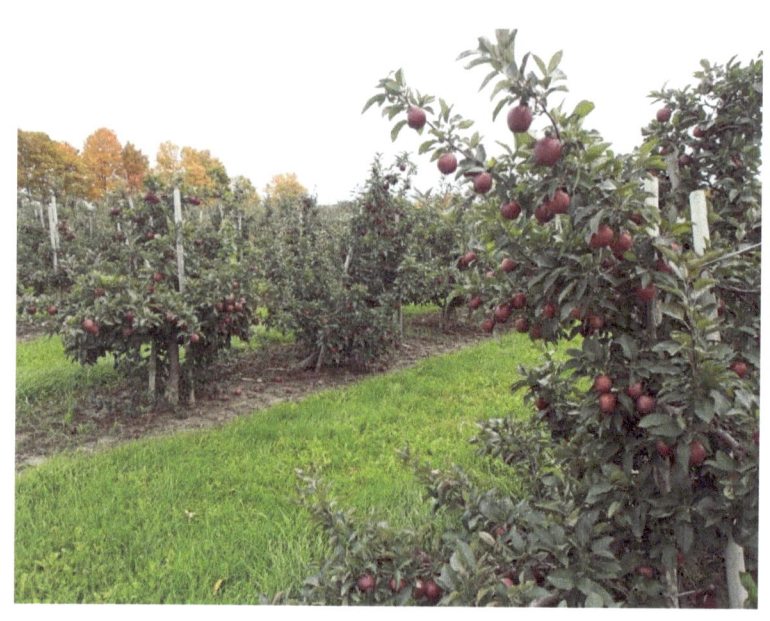

Apple orchard and fall colors

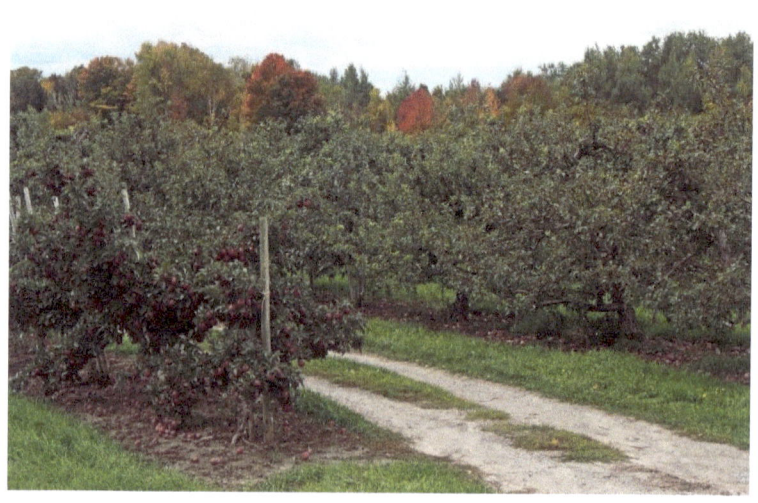

Rice Lake
Steamboats began to ply Rice Lake in 1832 and by the 1860s they regularly called at the dock meeting passengers and freight enroute between Cobourg and Peterborough.

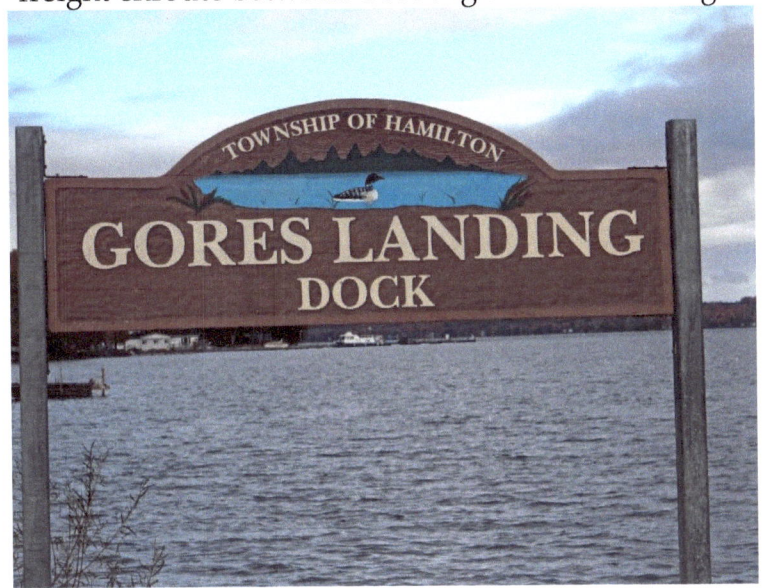

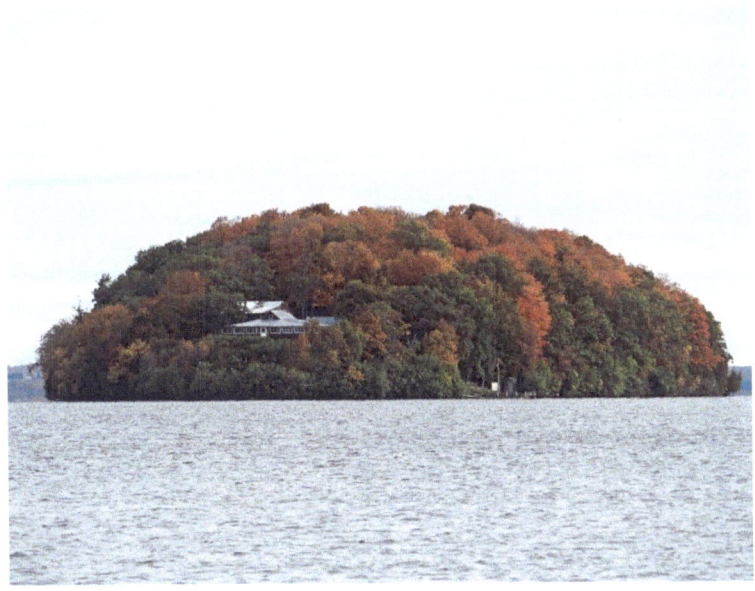

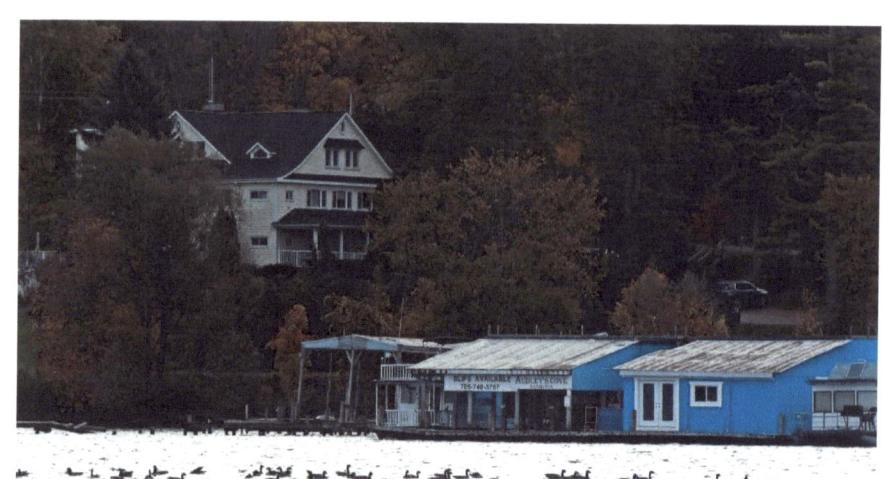
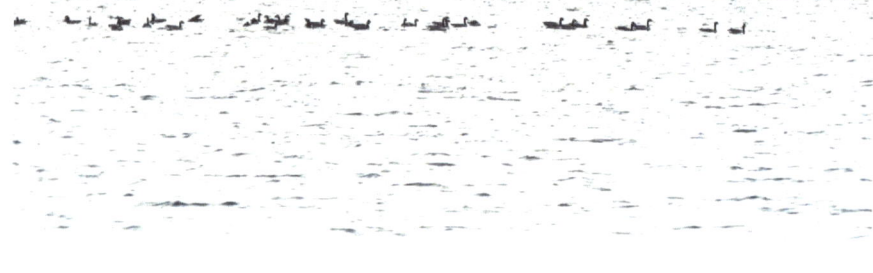

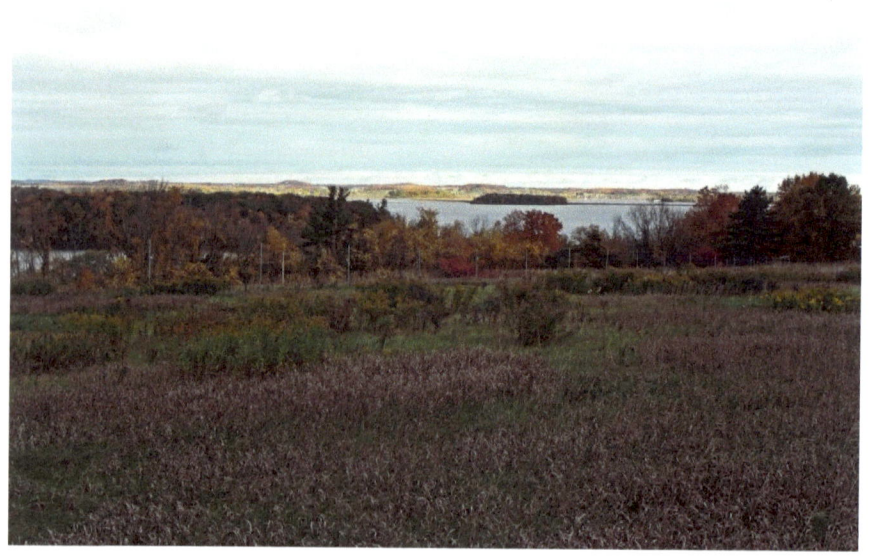

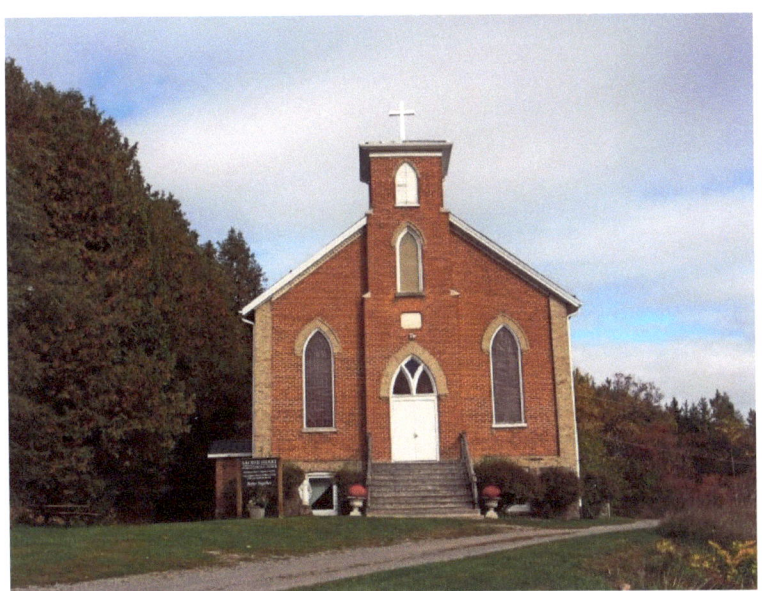

494 Bethesda Road North - Presbyterian Church A.D. 1882 – now Sacred Heart Roman Catholic Church, Mission of Hastings

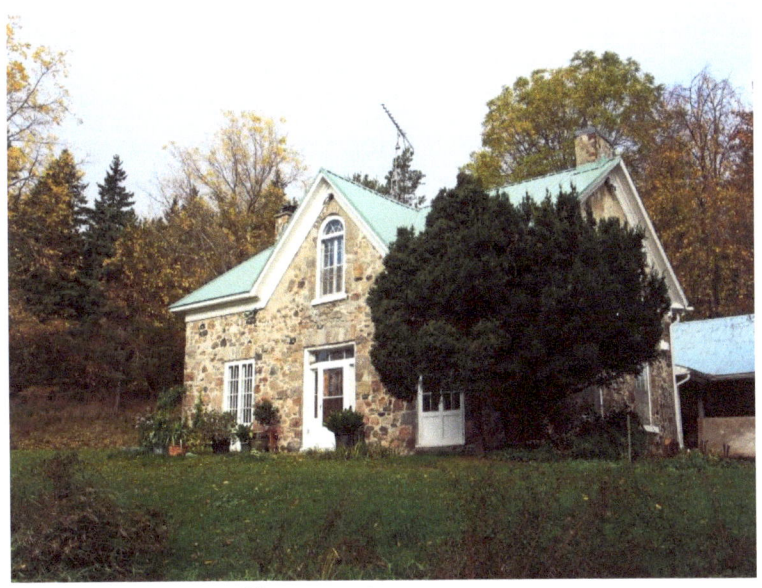

Former stone manse

Castleton

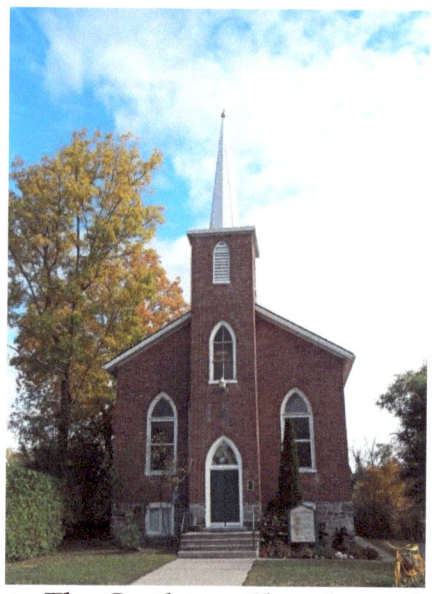

1815 Percy Street - The Castleton Church was built in 1865 by Wesleyan Methodists, and it continued to serve the community's spiritual needs 100 years later on its centenary, and it continues to thrive today, 151 years later. Built for $1,600.00, the church owed only $200.00 on the day of its opening and thanks to a collection taken that very day, the Castleton congregation could boast that their new church was debt free.

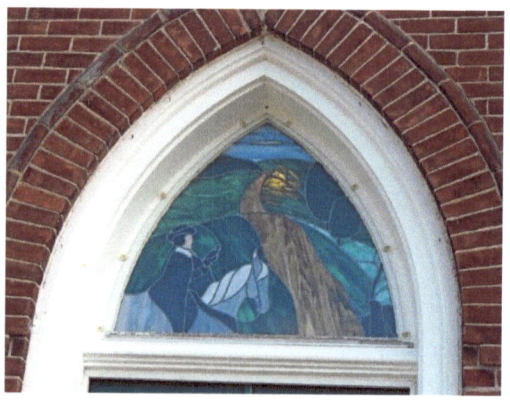

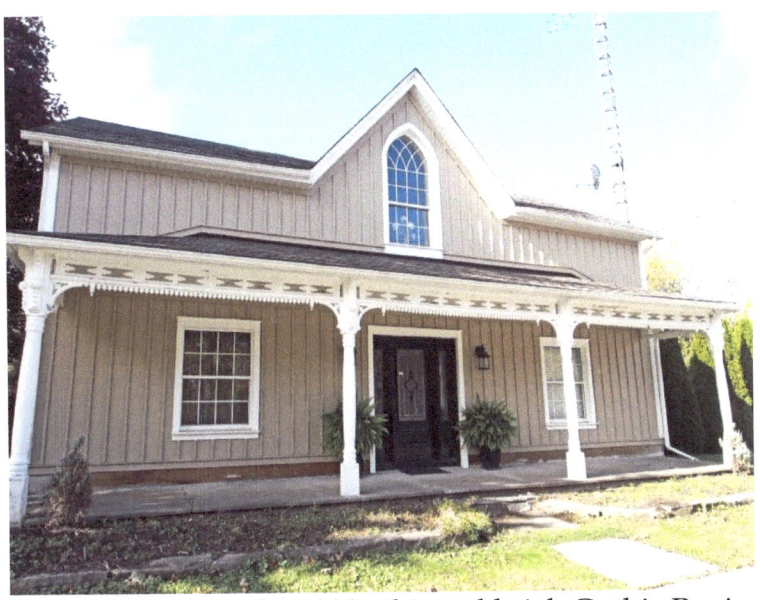

1804 Percy Street - In the 1880s this red brick Gothic Revival cottage with its multi-paned lancet window, was home to Michael John Doyle, an agent and assessor. Doyle was a former reeve of Cramahe Township as well as Warden of the United Counties of Durham and Northumberland. Influenced by the spirited political discussions in her childhood home, Doyle's daughter Iva, later Mrs. Howard Fallis, became Canada's first Conservative female Senator, in 1935, under Prime Minister R.B. Bennett. (The house was covered in siding in 2015).

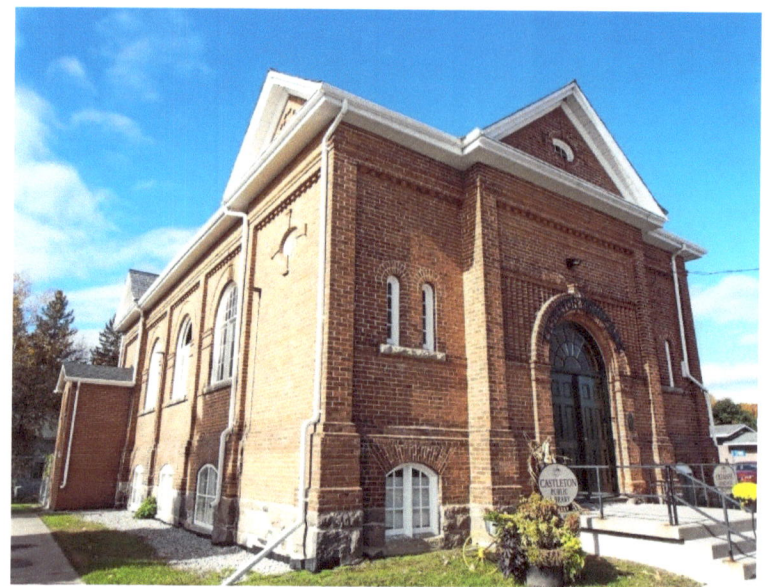

1780 Percy Street - The Crown Patent for the land upon which the Castleton Town Hall stands, was issued to the Canada Company in 1830. Sixty years later it was determined that Castleton was sufficiently established to require a town hall, and the Township of Cramahe bought the lot in 1892 for $150.00. The building was completed in 1893 by George Crowe of Trenton, at a cost of $3,900.00. The municipal office, jail cell, vault and Council Chambers were located downstairs. A concert hall with the original balcony is still situated on the upper floor.

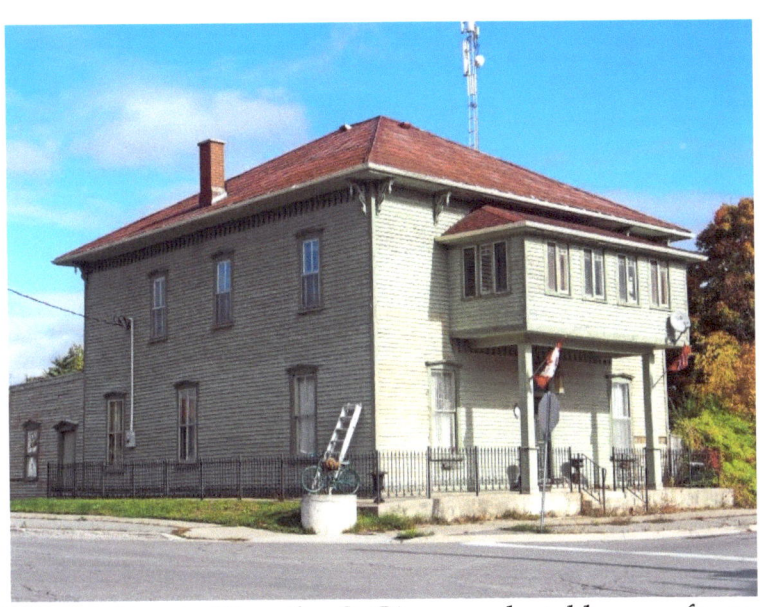

1777 Percy Street - Timothy S. Giroux, a hotel keeper from Norham, built this "frontier" styled building in the 1890s. The Oriental Hotel, which was also known as the Temperance, Union and Castleton Hotels over its lifetime, was host to traveling salesmen, bankers and entertainers. In the 1920s, the then Union Hotel charged 50 cents a meal and 1 dollar a night for lodging. At one time, the Oriental became home to the Canadian Imperial Bank of Commerce and the township library. It is now a private residence.

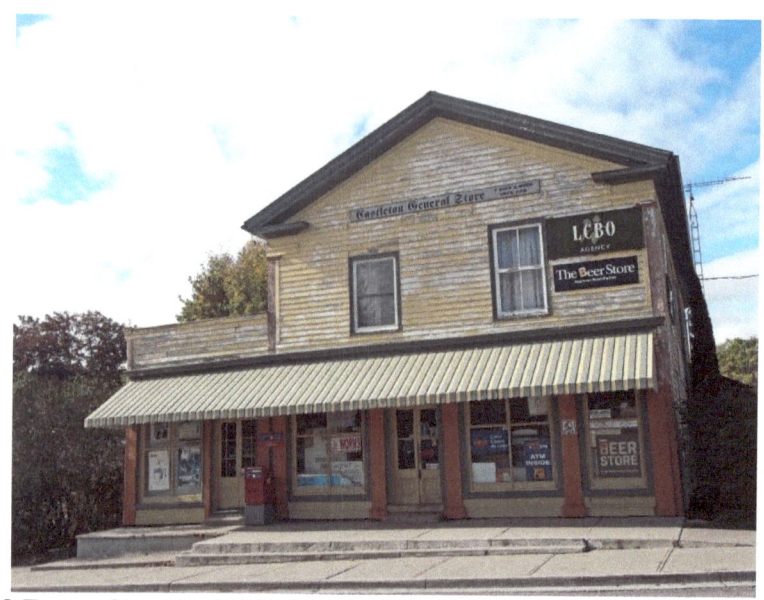

1768 Percy Street - G.W. Pinnock is listed as a general merchant in Castleton, in the 1865 Gazetteer. The Castleton General Store was built about that time and Pinnock operated it for twenty-five years until it was sold to the Newman Family in 1890. Newman ran the store under the name The Newman Company until 1976, when it changed hands again. The store operates to this day and still contains some of the original counters and display cases. It is renowned for its summer lineups for ice cream.

Wicklow

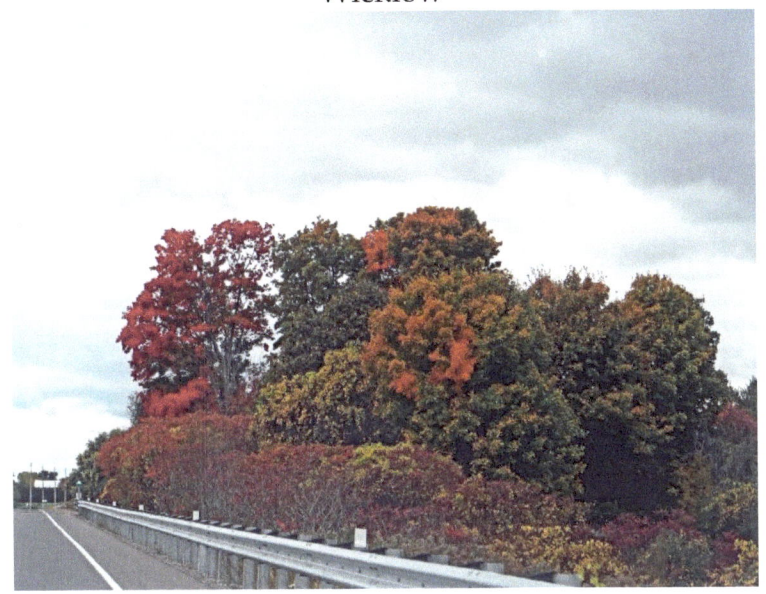

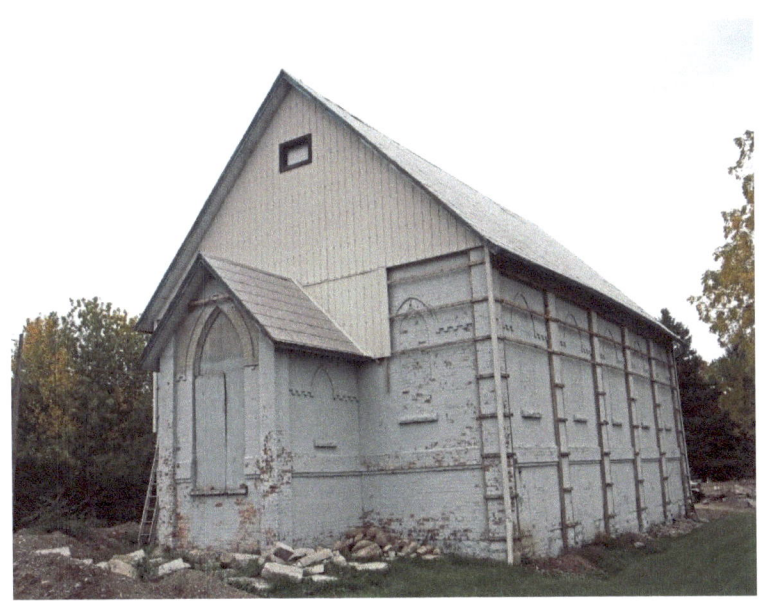

Wicklow Methodist Church – A.D. 1896

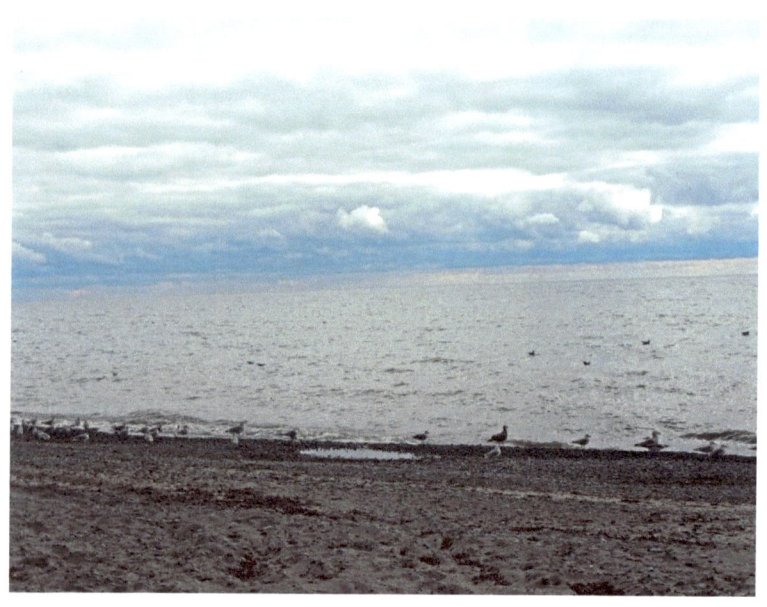

Wicklow Beach on Lake Ontario

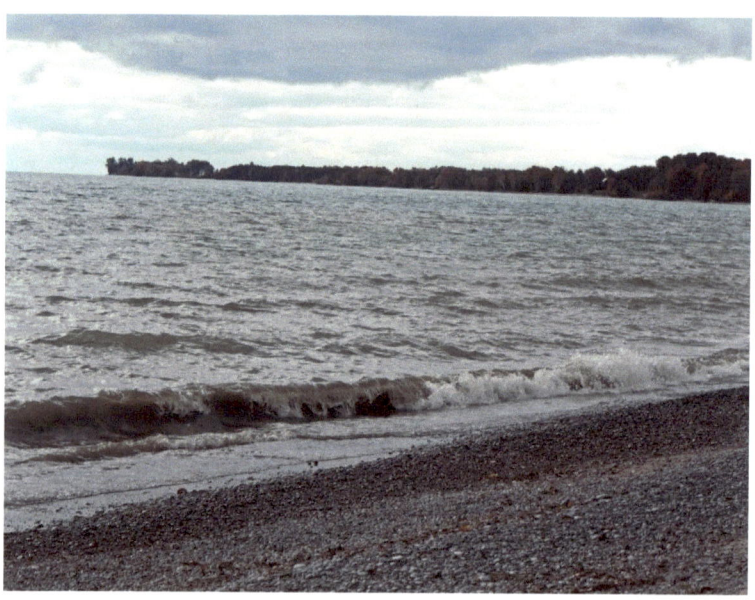

King City – King Township Museum

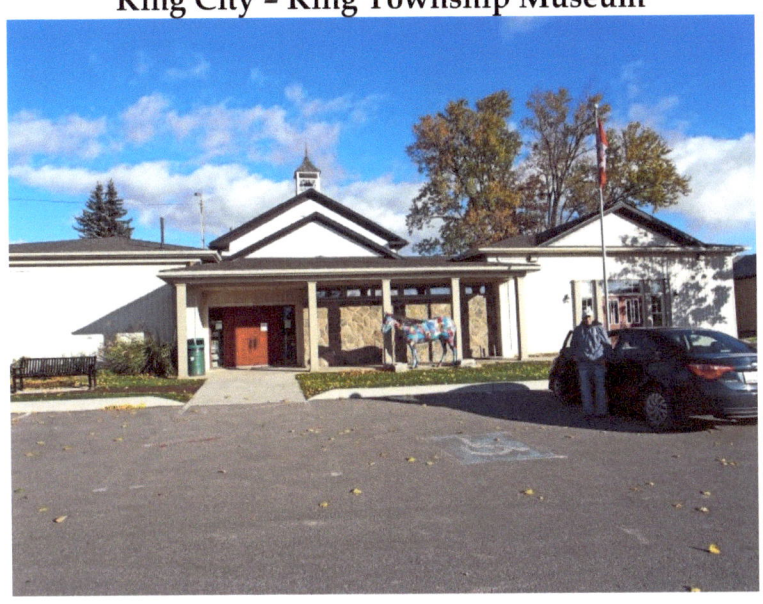

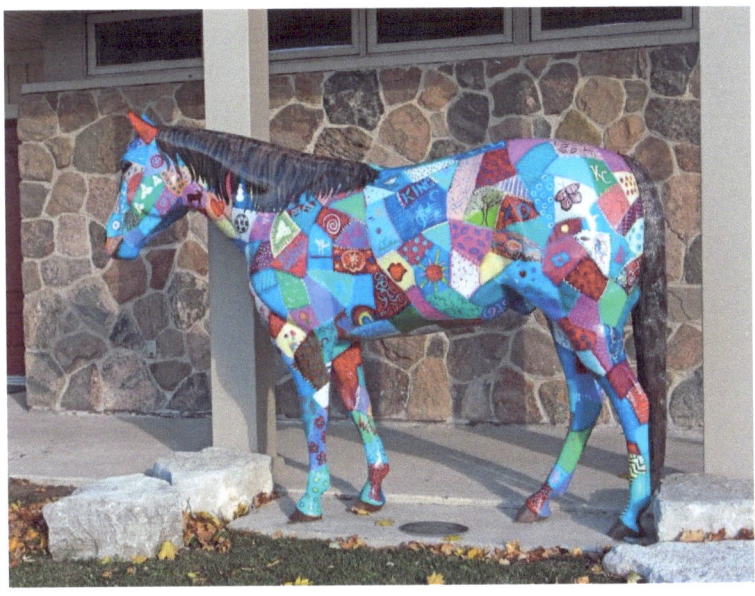

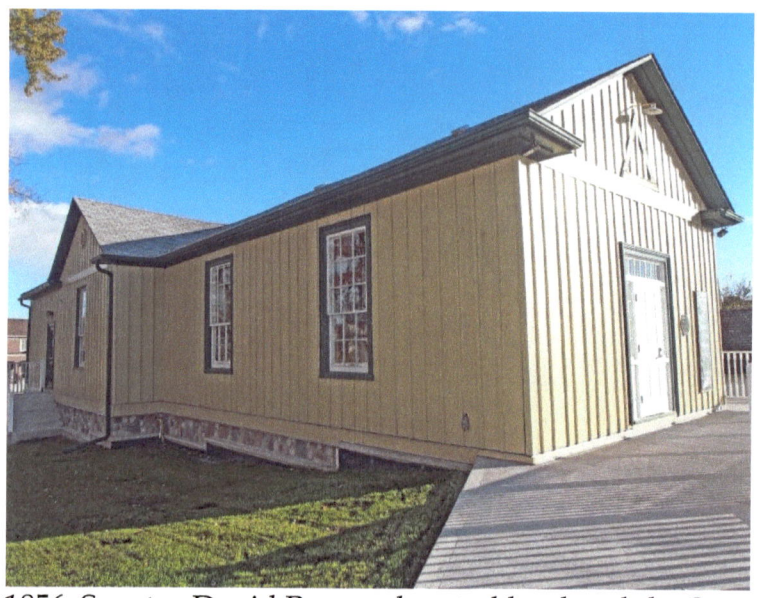

In 1856, Senator David Reesor donated land and the Sons of Temperance erected Laskay Temperance Hall which opened January 1, 1859. From 1914-1988 it was operated by the *Laskay Women's Institute*. In 1989 the hall was restored by the Laskay community supported by the Township of King and the province of Ontario.

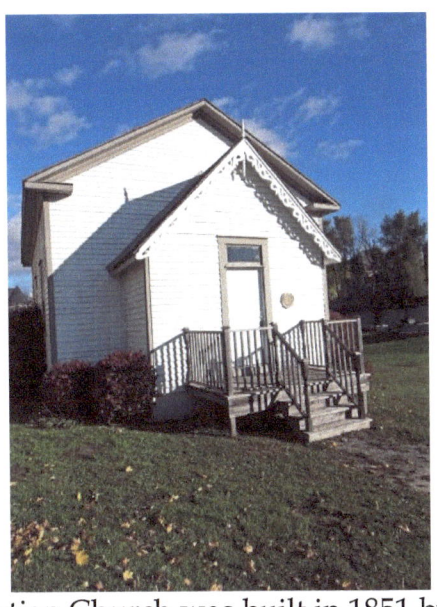

The King Christian Church was built in 1851 by a group from the Sharon Temple Quakers (Children of Peace) on an acre of land donated by Thomas Ramsden. The church and the adjacent burial ground served the community of Kettleby until 1931 when the congregation joined the Baptist Convention and the building renamed King Immanuel Baptist Church. A diminishing congregation led to its closure in 1978 and it was moved to this location in 1982.

The Toronto Carrying-Place Trail was a major portage route in Ontario linking Lake Ontario with Lake Simcoe and the northern Great Lakes. From Lake Ontario, the trail ran northward along the eastern bank of the Humber River. It forked at Woodbridge, with one path crossing the east branch of the Humber and running along the west side of the river to the vicinity of Kleinburg, where it crossed the river again. This trail was probably used during the seasons when the water was low enough to ford. The other path of the fork followed the east side of the river and angled cross-country to King Creek, joining the other fork before crossing the river near Nobleton about fifty kilometres north of Lake Ontario. From there it runs north over the Oak Ridges Moraine to the western branch of the Holland River, and from there northeast into Lake Simcoe about eighty kilometres north.

Once into Lake Simcoe, the trail continues north through straits on the north end of the lake into Lake Couchiching. These straits are an important fishing area and give rise to the name Toronto, as this is "the place where the trees grow over the water". The First Nations peoples had planted trees in the narrows between the lakes to act as a weir to catch fish. From there the trail follows the Severn River into Georgian Bay.

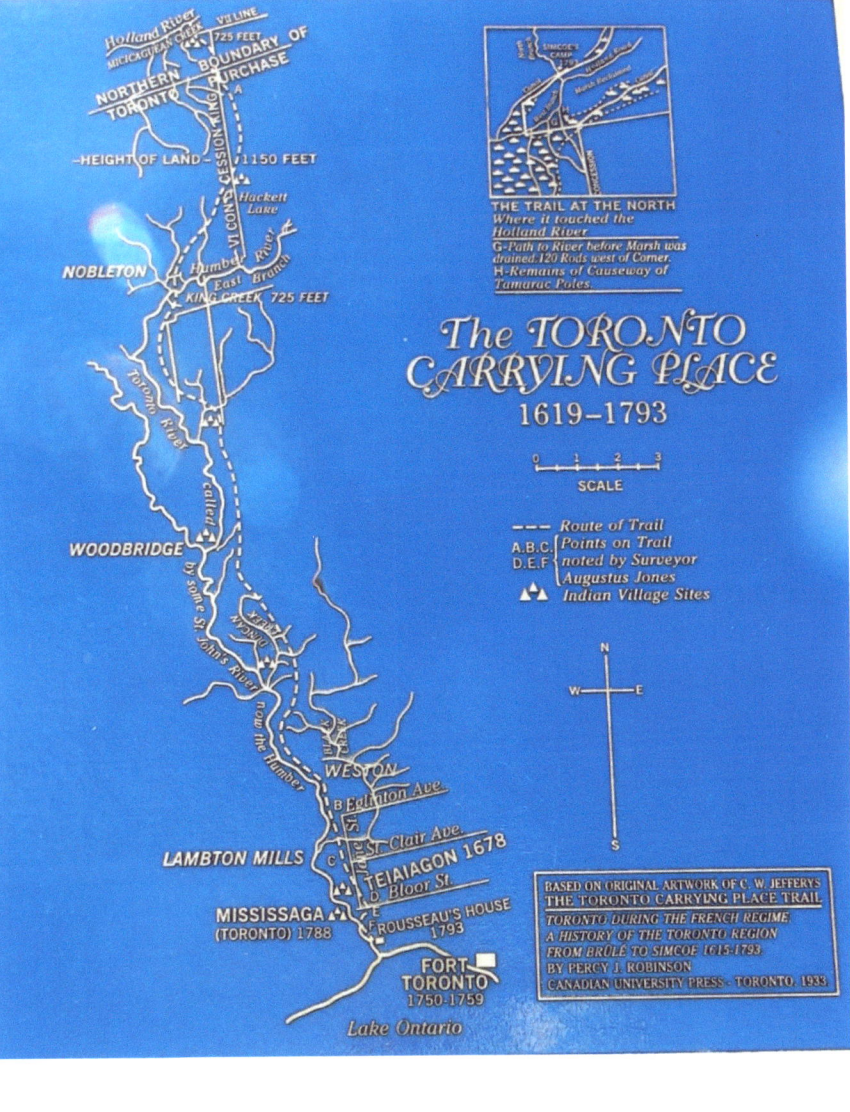

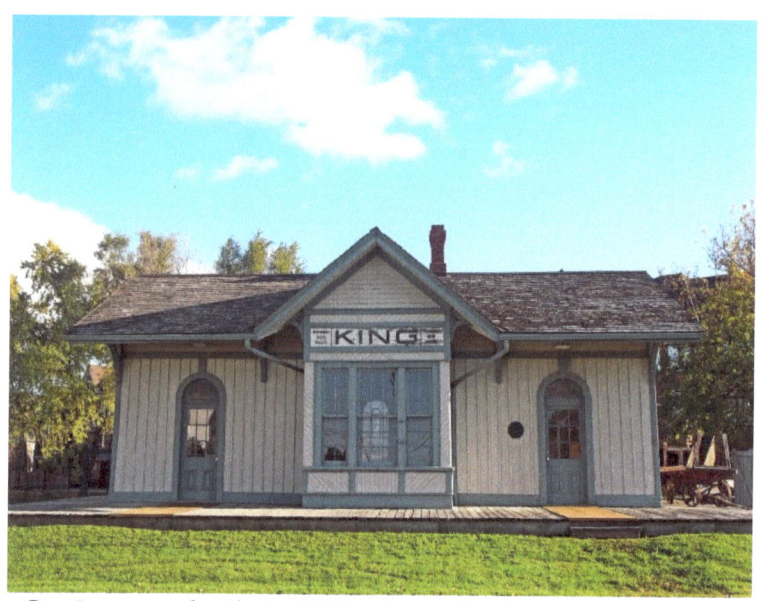

King Station was built in 1852 along the Northern Railway to serve *Springhill* (now King City). It was moved in 1989 to the grounds of the King Township Museum. It is believed to be the oldest surviving railway station in Canada.

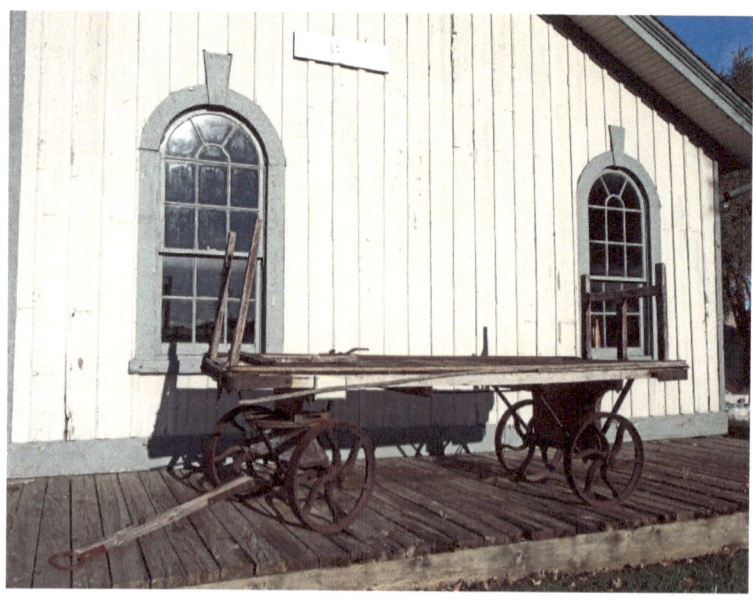

Nobleton

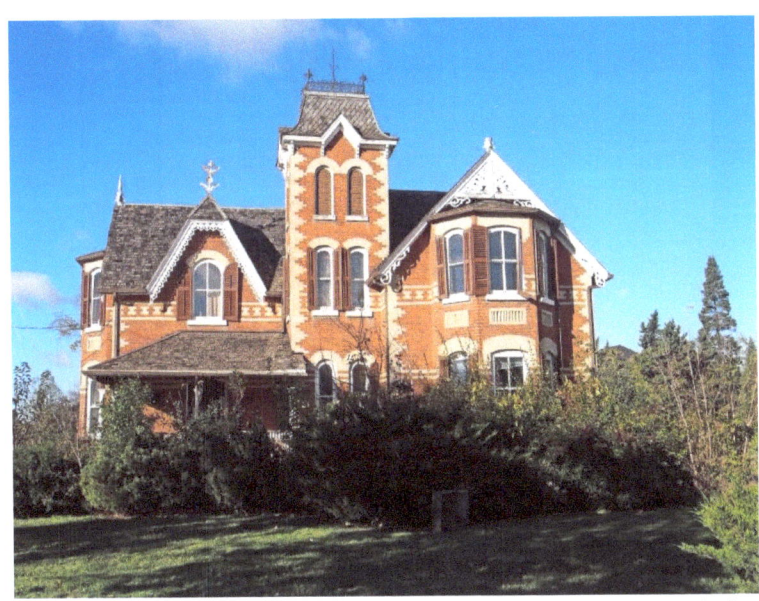

6012 King Road – Hambly House – c. 1884 – It was originally built of logs but was rebuilt after a fire at the corner of Highway 27 and King Road.

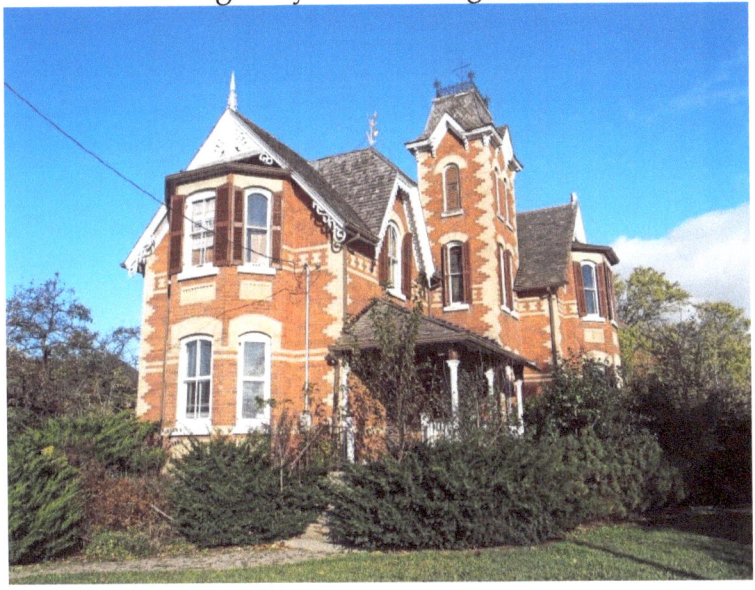

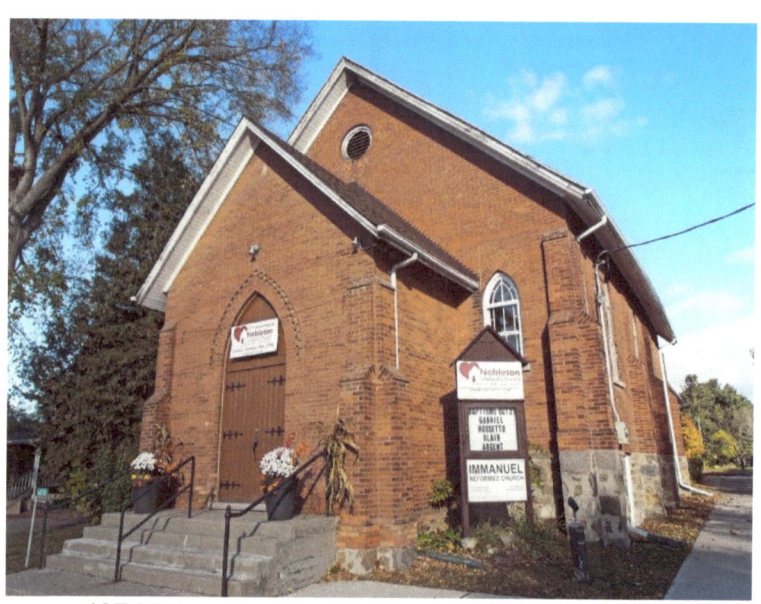

6076 King Road – Nobleton United Church

The first church in the Nobleton area was a Wesleyan Methodist, which was built in 1845, atop the hill, adjacent to the old cemetery, on the north side of King Road about a half mile west of Hwy 27. This site later became the original pipe style water tower which was later removed. The church was thus referred to as "The Church on the Hill". The original pioneer Methodist congregation consisted of two small congregations which later merged with the Wesleyan Methodist in 1874 and 1884, to form one main congregation.

The Church on the Hill was taken down and much of the material was used to construct a new Methodist Church later to become the United Church, on its present site. The original land consisted of a ¼ acre parcel purchased from Mrs. James Adams, the widow of the late Rev. James Adams. In later years land was donated to the church, for expansion of a septic system, by Thomas Chapman. The construction of the present church has been done in several phases. The excavation of the original basement and erection of the main part of the church was completed by "bees", dug by hand with much labour donated by members of the congregation. The cornerstone laying took place on May 25, 1896.

1925   The Methodist Church became the Nobleton United Church, part of a three point charge consisting of Kleinburg, Central and Nobleton.

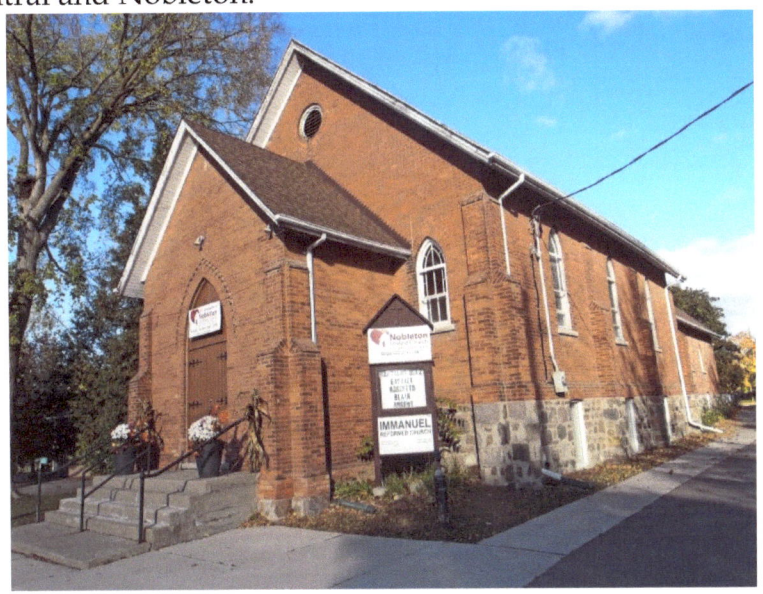

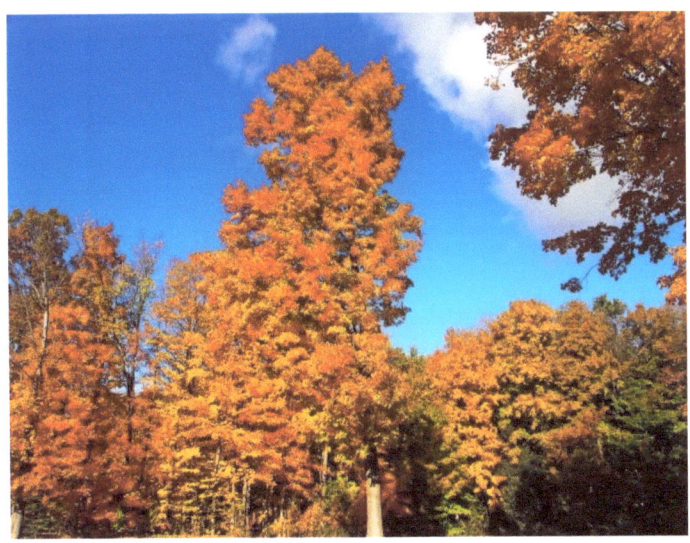

Other Books by Barbara Raue

Coins of Gold
Arrows, Indians and Love
The Life and Times of Barbara
The Cromwell Family Book
Laura Secord Discovered
Daddy Where Are You?

Montana Series
Book 1: Montana Dream
Book 2: Life on the Montana Frontier
Book 3: Montana to Boston and Back
Book 4: Montana Sons Go to War
Book 5: Montana Sons Return from War

Visit Barbara's website to view all of her books
http://barbararaue.ca

© 2018 by Barbara Raue - All the photos in this book have been taken with my cameras. I own the rights to them.